TALK, TALK, TALK JESUS
Is that all she's good for?

Yes! Let us exalt His name together!

Rosellen Lewis

TALK, TALK, TALK JESUS
Is that all she's good for?

IRENE LEWERS
with
Rosellen Lewis

New Leaf Press
P.O. BOX 311, GREEN FOREST, AR 72638

SECOND EDITION

Typesetting by: Type-O-Graphics, Springfield, MO.

Library of Congress Catalog Number: 90-61751
ISBN: 0-89221-184-9

DEDICATION

To the glory of God our Father
the Lord Jesus Christ
and the Holy Spirit
in thanksgiving
for His love
His mercy
and
His grace.

"Since my youth, O God, you have taught me, and to this day I declare your marvelous deeds. Even when I am old and gray, do not forsake me, O God, till I declare Your might to all who are to come. Your righteousness reaches to the skies, O God, you who have done great things. Who, O God, is like you?" (Ps. 71:17-19; NIV).

ACKNOWLEDGMENTS

When the Lord told Jeremiah to write in a book the things He had spoken to him, Jeremiah called upon his friend Baruch to do the writing as he recounted it to him (Jer. 36:4). Many thanks, in the name of Jesus, to Rosellen Lewis and also to Charles and Kathy Self, Bob Shatswell and others for their help and encouragement, as well as to my husband, Bill, for his love and support.

Table of Contents

FOREWORD

It is a privilege to introduce to you Mrs. Irene Lewers and this testimony from her life and relationship with God. Irene has been a faithful and fruitful member of Calvary Community Church. We have had many opportunities to hear of the special and unique ways the Holy Spirit has worked in her life. The most special fact of all is the character and integrity the Holy Spirit has produced in Irene's life. This has been accomplished so that God might receive greater glory and the work of the Kingdom might be established in the hearts of men, women, and young people around the world.

We hope that you will enjoy reading *Talk, Talk, Talk Jesus*, which speaks of the work God's Spirit has accomplished in one simple and faith-minded young woman from Kona, Hawaii. More importantly, we hope that you will be encouraged to believe that God will work faithfully in your life through the power of the Holy Spirit. My prayer is that every word of this testimony will point you closer to Jesus and you can laugh, cry, and rejoice as God weaves His thread of faith in your life today.

Pastor Gerald L. Fry
Calvary Community Church
San Jose, California

PSALM 145 (NIV)

"I will exalt you, my God the King; I will praise your name for ever and ever.

Every day I will praise you and extol your name for ever and ever.

Great is the Lord and most worthy of praise; his greatness no one can fathom.

One generation will commend your works to another; they will tell of your mighty acts.

They will speak of the glorious splendor of your majesty, and I will meditate on your wonderful works.

They will tell of the power of your awesome works, and I will proclaim your great deeds.

They will celebrate your abundant goodness and joyfully sing of your righteousness.

The Lord is gracious and compassionate, slow to anger and rich in love.

The Lord is good to all; he has compassion on all he has made.

All you have made will praise you, O Lord; your saints will extol you.

They will tell of the glory of your kingdom and speak of your might,

so that all men may know of your mighty acts and the glorious splendor of your kingdom.

Your kingdom is an everlasting kingdom, and your dominion endures through all generations.

The Lord is faithful to all his promises and loving toward all he has made.

The Lord upholds all those who fall and lifts up all who are bowed down.

The eyes of all look to you, and you give them their food at the proper time.

You open your hand and satisfy the desires of every living thing.

The Lord is righteous in all his ways and loving toward all he has made.

The Lord is near to all who call on him, to all who call on him in truth.

He fulfills the desires of those who fear him; he hears their cry and saves them.

The Lord watches over all who love him, but all the wicked he will destroy.

My mouth will speak in praise of the Lord. Let every creature praise his holy name for ever and ever.''

PREFACE
The Birthing of a Book

Talk, Talk, Talk Jesus. I stared at the title of the book on a shelf in the bookstore at our church.

"What an odd title," I remember thinking to myself, but for some reason I did not pick it up to look at it that day back in 1974.

A week or so later I had one of those early morning dreams. It was short but vivid—

I was preparing breakfast for my husband Bill when the phone rang. He answered it, then handed it to me saying, "It's our pastor, Pastor Fry. He wants to speak to you."

"Yes, hello, Pastor."

"Hello, Irene." Without further greeting, he asked, "Irene, have you read ...?" and he named a certain book. "Also," he added, *"Talk, Talk, Talk Jesus?"*

"No, I haven't read either one," I replied.

"Read them," he said.

I waited for him to say more, but there was only a long silence. I finally hung up the phone.

When I woke up, I recalled having seen the little book titled, *Talk, Talk, Talk Jesus* distinctly remembering every detail of its colorful cover. As soon as the bookstore opened that morning I called to inquire about the two books Pastor Fry had named in the dream. Marge, the manager of the bookstore, answered the phone.

"Yes," she said, "we have the first one you named, but not the other one. I've never even heard of *Talk, Talk, Talk Jesus*."

"But Marge," I protested, "I saw it right there in the bookstore just the other day." I proceeded to describe it to her in detail, and the shelf on which I had seen it. Marge was familiar with every book in the store and would certainly remember that one if it were there. I told her about the dream.

"What I'll do," she said, "is consult the publishers' lists and check with a couple of them by phone today when I place orders with them, then call you back."

True to her word she called back in the afternoon sounding rather puzzled.

"Irene," she said, "not only is *Talk, Talk, Talk Jesus* not listed, no one has ever heard of it. Maybe this is a book someone is writing that the Lord wants you to read. There may be a message in it for you."

I was dumbfounded for I KNEW positively that I had seen that book. It was NOT a dream. How strange. There was no explaining it. I gave up trying and mentally set it aside as another new, yet baffling, experience.

Years before, in Honolulu, I had shared some of my experiences with the Lord with a school teacher friend.

"Write it down!" she would say again and again. "These things don't belong only to you. They belong to anyone who will listen!"

Others have urged me in similar fashion but I never took them seriously. Me? Write a book?! Ridiculous! Absurd! Impossible! You have to be joking.

However, when the Lord clearly spoke to my heart in 1976 that I was to write a book I could not ignore it. "Lord, You can't mean me. You know I can't write well."

Have you ever argued with the Lord? If so, have you ever won an argument with Him? No? Well, neither did I. He did with me as He did with Moses—He promised to give me a helper. That was all. There was no word about what to write or when.

Two more years slipped by. It was in 1978 when our Lord showed me just as clearly that the book I was to write was to be titled *Talk, Talk, Talk Jesus*. It would be a small book and the cover would be like the one I remembered seeing in the bookstore.

But how could that be? Surely such a book had already been written! Besides, I knew full well that there was no way I could write a book on my own. Gently, the Lord reminded me that what is impossible with men is possible with God. He never requires the impossible of us, but always makes a way when we are willing to obey. When His way involves another person, He can be trusted to make His will known to that one also—in this case, Rosellen the following year.

In 1980, while ministering in Kona, Hawaii, I stayed with my youngest sister Betty and told her about being directed to write a book.

"The title will be *Talk, Talk, Talk Jesus*," I said.

Betty gasped, "Oh, Sis, do you know that is **exactly** what people used to say behind your back years ago—'Is that all she's good for, to talk, talk, talk Jesus?' "

No, I didn't know that.

Still, I dragged my feet. Then one day while visiting in the home of a friend, another visitor, a woman I had barely met and spoken with only briefly, suddenly turned to me. "Irene," she said firmly, "you are writing a book. God has already given you the title. You must get it done quickly. **You must do it now!**"

I could hardly believe my ears. I stood awe-struck! We had only just met and she knew almost nothing about me. Surely, the Lord was speaking to me through this woman. It was up to me, now, to obey His word in complete dependence upon the Holy Spirit to show me clearly what things were to be written and what things were not.

It is easy for me to identify with the apostle John in the concluding words of his gospel record: "There are also many other things which Jesus did, the which, if they should be written every one, I suppose that even the world itself could not contain the books which should be written" (John 21:25). Clearly, it was necessary for John to record only what the Holy Spirit had selectively shown to him.

So, in like sense, what is written here is an abbreviated account of one life that God turned around and turned toward Him as He began to touch my heart while I was a young girl. Step by step He very patiently taught and led me, by means of visions and dreams, even before He could do so by means of the Scriptures. There is no way I can thank Him enough as He continues to teach, to correct, to guide, to encourage, and to fill me with His love, joy, strength, and peace regardless of the circumstances life brings.

Who knows how bitter our trials may be—and, indeed, are even now in some parts of the world? The time may come when some of us will not have the strengthening support of fellow believers or even the Bible, but only the Lord Jesus who promised never ever to leave us or forsake us. But He is sufficient and forever able to communicate the reality of His love, His grace, His power, His presence and His will to any open heart. **I know**, for that's what He has done in my life.

The days in which we live are perilous ones, what Scripture calls "the end times." Truly it is the sunset hour. More than ever before we need the confidence of knowing that no matter what happens, no matter where we are, OUR GOD LIVES. He goes before us, stands beside us, and watches over us. We need have no fear if we belong to Him who loves us with an everlasting love.

In sharing this portion of my life with you, it is my hope and my prayer that your own heart will be encouraged and your confidence strengthened in the reality and power of the living God in our midst. All praise and honor to His glorious name!

—Irene Lewers

"Now, go, write it on a tablet before them and inscribe it on a scroll, that it may serve in the time to come as a witness forever" (Isa. 30:8; NASB).

1

THE HEAVENLY MUSIC

The night was like any other soft, clear night in Kona, Hawaii. All was quiet, everyone sleeping soundly in the Jenkins home out among the coffee fields, where my older sister Alice and I shared a bedroom.

The sound of music wakened me. Was I dreaming? No, I could hear it coming from somewhere outside. Slipping out of bed I stepped over to the unscreened window and leaned out to see where such beautiful music might be coming from. In the dim night light I could see nothing unusual. The sky was full of stars shining with all the brilliance so typical of a Hawaiian night sky. The music seemed to be coming from all over the heavens. I caught my breath, for never in my life had I heard such music. It was beautiful, so very beautiful. I stood listening, enthralled and touched to the very depths of my being.

"Alice must hear this too," I thought to myself and excitedly shook her awake.

"Listen," I whispered, "just listen, Alice. There's music all over the heavens!"

She wakened enough to protest, "Oh...Irene, you're hearing things."

"No," I insisted, "there's music. Don't you hear it?"

Alice propped her head up on one elbow to listen. "I don't hear a thing," she said after a moment.

I had stepped back to the window to listen. "Just listen," I urged her. "It's so beautiful! Listen!"

But Alice was hearing nothing and did not appreciate being roused from sleep in the middle of the night by her ten-year-old sister to listen to music she could not hear. Enough was enough. By now she was very much disturbed and began calling out for Mother.

In some alarm at being wakened from a sound sleep, Mother came running down the hall. "What is it? What's the matter?" she asked as she came hurrying into our room.

"Irene says she hears music coming from all over the heavens," my sister told her.

Mother listened, but could hear nothing like music. Quickly I moved back to the window and listened, but the music was gone! The night was still.

"Irene, did you hear music?" There was an edge to Mother's voice as she asked the question. "Are you sure?"

"Yes, I did," I assured her. "I heard music. I heard beautiful music."

"At two o'clock in the morning!" she exclaimed. "You just get right back into bed."

Obediently, I climbed back into bed, but could not possibly get back to sleep. I was so filled with the beauty and wonder of what I had heard. At the same time I was aware of an extraordinary gentle warmth throughout my whole being, and there was an inner excitement which kept me lying awake until morning.

All of us children had regular chores to do, one of which was to get up early and make coffee for my parents, to serve to them in their bedroom. It happened to be my turn that morning. However, that morning my mother got up, came into the kitchen where I was preparing the coffee, and began questioning me.

"Irene, did you really hear music last night?"

"Yes, I did."

"What did it sound like?"

"Oh, Mother, it sounded like a thousand harps!"

"My foolish child, you have never in your life heard a harp."

That was true; I had not. At the time I didn't know why I had used that description. It was to be many years before an understanding would come.

Our home was surrounded by acres of coffee fields near Kona on the big island of Hawaii. The house was a modest frame building with a galvanized roof typical of many older homes in Hawaii in that year of 1932. My parents and the five of us children had moved there from Honolulu a year before. My mother's parents had emigrated to Hawaii from Portugal as young children and now lived only a few miles away. In accordance with the European tradition, my grandparents still exercised some authority in family matters.

When others in the family learned about my hearing music in the heavens in the middle of the night, it was a source of much concern and discussion. It was a serious matter, and one to be considered by the family. So my grandparents were called in as well as an uncle and a school-teacher aunt.

"Well, I'll tell you," said my aunt, "it could be that music is in the air and it hit the galvanized roof."

With that wonderful, logical turn of mind men so often have, my father countered, "Well, then, the roof would be singing all the time and everyone would have heard it. Besides," he reasoned, "the house is not wired for electricity and no one has a radio."

One by one every conceivable possibility was ruled out.

There is an element of fear in the unknown. Because there was no reasonable explanation for the music I heard, my parents strictly forbid me to tell anyone. They would punish me severely if I did, for people would surely think I was crazy.

My parents watched me very closely for several days after that to be sure I was not losing my mind. In much fear, especially of my father, I said nothing to anyone. I just tucked away the strange and beautiful experience inside.

One thing was sure: the music was real. I heard it! Why didn't Mother and Alice hear it too? Where did it come from? Would I ever hear it again? Then that strange, soft warmth and buoyancy inside. What was it? What did it mean?

Questions—lots of questions, without answers...

Eventually, I came to understand that the lovely warmth I had felt was just one of the ways the Lord has of manifesting His presence and one which I was to experience many times. Some of you have known it in your own lives; some have not. Who can say how many various ways God has of making His presence real? He deals differently with different people as well as in different ways with the same person at different times. None of us should look for Him to work the same way in our lives that He has in others. Nor should we reject a beautiful, uplifting experience just because we don't understand it, whether the experience has been our own or someone else's.

You may ask, "What about the music you heard filling the night sky? Did you ever hear it again? Do you have any understanding of it now?"

No, I never heard it again. Yes, a measure of insight and understanding did come much later and very unexpectedly.

It was 1979, forty-seven years after I had heard the glorious heavenly music, when my friend, Rosellen, was in a Sunday morning Bible class. The instructor had referred to a verse in the book of Job where it says, "the morning stars sang together" (Job 38:7), suggesting that the writer of the book showed himself to have remarkable understanding of the creation and meant the words to be taken literally. In Job's day, men knew nothing about wave lengths, about frequencies of light and of sound. Today we know that light travels approximately 186,000 miles per second. We also know that if it is slowed down sufficiently, it becomes sound.

Rosellen was immediately reminded of the heavenly music I had told her of hearing in 1932. Suddenly, it came to her that she **knew** what that music was.

"Irene, that's what you heard!" she told me in great excitement as soon as she could call and explain what had happened in the class. "Remember? It was two o'clock in the morning when you heard the music. 'The morning stars sang together' and the Lord allowed you to hear them!"

As Rosellen spoke, I too, knew in my heart that what God had shown her was true. What an amazing, wonderful God we have! Together we praised Him and thanked Him for the insight He had given us through Scripture.

It makes one wonder…how often are we inclined to "spiritualize" or even dismiss a Scripture we do not understand instead of believing it to be literally true? God help us!

It is one of God's principles that "every fact is to be confirmed by the testimony of two or three witnesses" (2 Cor. 13:1; NASB). The next one came from the scientific community through a popular monthly magazine in March, 1982. It held a brief report on the sounds recorded by an instrument on the Voyager II spacecraft. The instrument picked up radio waves which were then rigged to a micro-computer and music synthesizer. Such radio sound comes from what is called solar wind, the current of electrically charged particles that are continuously flowing out from the sun. In a planet's magnetic field those particles vibrate much like the string on a musical instrument when it is plucked. A great variety of celestial music has thus been recorded.

"What did the music sound like?" my mother had asked.

"Like a thousand harps," I had replied, not then knowing why.

It was to be exactly fifty years before I knew. Believe me, that was exciting. We have an exciting God, One who is faithful and true. He **will** validate whatever is of Him, **always** in accord with His written Word...even if if takes fifty years to do so!

Truly, "The heavens are telling the glory of God; and the firmament is declaring the work of His hands" (Ps. 19:1; NASB).

2

MEETING THE CHRIST
OF THE CROSS

As a child I really did not know the Lord Jesus. I had heard of Him, had learned the Lord's Prayer and loved to sing carols at Christmas time. Somehow I knew that God is and that He is good, but that was about all.

Our family did not attend church although my Mother "belonged" to one. My parents were morally upright, good, hardworking people who tried to be good parents. Surely, that never is an easy job. They were private people, and whatever went on in our home was always regarded as strictly private. We did not "neighbor" with nor confide in people outside the family.

Dad was very much a man of his word. By precept and example we children learned that promises must be kept. We had to personally apologize to the other person if it became impossible to keep our word. Dad was a very strict disciplinarian and I was rather afraid of him, but I am deeply grateful for such training.

Being a sensitive child, often, when I felt especially hurt, I would go down to the garden and pick sweet potato vines. That may sound like a strange way for a child to nurse her hurts, but we used to feed certain branches to the rabbits we kept. A natural spring there made it a cool and refreshing spot to stop and rest. So, with my bag of sweet potato vines, I would sit there and talk to God, pouring out my heart to Him, and be comforted. Sometimes, I would lift my face and throw kisses to Him.

It was just a simple, natural thing to talk to God that way. I didn't think of it as praying. Indeed, I knew very little about prayer. In our home we did not even "say grace" at meal times. I had never heard of "grace" until I was about thirteen.

My oldest brother and I had been invited to stay for dinner at a friend's home. We had all taken our places around the table and sat down. "We'll have grace now," said our hostess from the head of the table. I remember looking around to see who and where Grace might be. Then a prayer was spoken for God's blessing on the food. How embarrassed I was! I could only hope it didn't show.

It was soon after hearing the beautiful heavenly music that another important event in my life took place. Mr. Akana, my school teacher, was also the school principal. It was shortly before Easter, and he had taken our class out on the lawn where we could gather around him under a tree. There was to be a school program on the last day before Easter vacation in which our class would participate.

"What would you like to sing for the Easter program?" he asked the class.

One of the girls suggested, "How about 'Alas and Did My Savior Bleed?' "

Mr. Akana nodded in agreement. "That's a good suggestion. Let me read the words to you. 'Alas, and did my Savior bleed? And did my Sovereign die? Would He devote that sacred head to such a worm as I?' "

The blank looks on some of our faces must have prompted him to say, "Let me explain to you, class." And he began to tell us about the sufferings of our Lord Jesus, about His crucifixion, and His resurrection as I had never heard it before. My heart broke as I listened.

After school I could hardly wait to get home and tell Mother what our teacher had said. I ran most of the two miles home, running so hard that my sides ached. Mother was in the kitchen preparing dinner when I burst into the house, out of breath, telling, as best I could, all that Mr. Akana had told us.

"Oh, Mother, I wish I had been there. I would have helped Jesus carry the cross."

She spun around to face me, both her eyes and her voice blazing. "Don't you ever say that again! Don't you ever even mention it!"

I was totally unprepared for Mother's response. Stunned and bewildered, I did not understand her reaction at all. But, of course, my dear Mother, herself, did not understand why I had spoken as I did. How rash I must have sounded to her. Her first impulse was to put a stop to such talk. Admittedly, my words were foolish words, but as a child, I didn't realize that. I sincerely believed what I had said.

Crushed and crying inside (where no one could see me), I quickly went to change clothes and feed the rabbits, pausing at the spring to talk to Jesus. Somehow, I knew He understood. To others, I obediently said nothing at all.

"He Himself bore our sins in His body on the cross, that we might die to sin and live to righteousness" (1 Pet. 2:24; NASB).

"And how shall they believe in Him whom they have not heard? And how shall they hear without a preacher?" (Rom. 10:14; NASB).

3

SUDDENLY, AN ADULT

"Freak!"

"Jackass!"

The children hee-hawed in derision. I was the object of their unmerciful teasing, especially the boys.

I was born with six toes on each foot, each of the last two being webbed together. In perennially warm, sunny Hawaii, we children either went barefoot or wore open-toed sandals, so the oddity of my six toes was obvious. Children are just naturally cruel and they unfailingly met me with jeers and taunts every time I entered the school yard.

"Mother, why," I implored her, "why wasn't I born with normal toes?"

"God made you that way," was her reply. "Just don't pay any attention to the teasing."

For me that was impossible. Children have always found that being different hurts, and I was no exception. The teasing made me even more sensitive and shy, especially with children my own age.

"Please," I began begging my parents, "let me leave school."

In Hawaii, in those days, children were not required to attend school beyond the sixth grade and so my parents agreed to let me quit when I finished sixth grade.

At home my parents gave me much more responsibility, including the care of the three youngest children who were then preschoolers. The added responsibilities undoubtedly had a maturing effect and in some ways I became old for my age. That was true of my physical development as well. In fact, I was embarrassed to tell anyone my true age because I both looked and felt much older.

By the time I turned fourteen I was ready to leave home and launch out on a life of my own. I asked my parents' permission to do so and they consented. Dad drove me by truck to Honakaa. From there I boarded a bus for Hilo, one hundred twenty miles away, to look for a job. Being old for my years, both in looks and home training, finding work would not be too difficult, and indeed, I soon found employment working at the hospital in Hilo.

Then it happened—I met Bill, my future husband. It was late December, just two months after arriving in Hilo, that a girlfriend and I went to a dance. How well I remember sitting on a bench against the wall and watching this good-looking young man crossing the dance floor and coming straight toward me. There was a bounce in his step and a light in his eyes as they met mine. Yes, there is such a thing as love at first sight! It happened to both of us. However, I would not allow him, a stranger, to take me home that evening.

It was a month later before we met again. It was at a dance where Bill was playing the bass viol in the orchestra. In the weeks that followed he came to see me frequently and I got to know him as a man of principle, with a warm heart, and lots of spunk. Bill was twenty-four, and he believed me when I told him I was nineteen.

Bill wanted to go to my parents for their consent to marry me, but I talked him out of it, not wanting him to know I was a mere fourteen and a half years old! So we were married in a simple civil ceremony in March, 1936, and told my parents by letter of our marriage. They lost no time in getting to Hilo! Because of my unwillingness, Dad himself finally had to tell Bill that I had deceived him about my age.

Oh! How awful I felt, how ashamed, and how sorry! I loved my husband dearly and tearfully pleaded with him for his forgiveness. That was a lot to ask, but Bill was a big enough man to grant it. We thank God that he did, for our marriage has proven its durability.

Our wedding picture March 4, 1936...I was fourteen years old.

"The steps of a good man are ordered by the Lord: and he delighteth in his way" (Ps. 37:23).

4

THE LORD OF LIFE

Our first daughter, Carol Ann, was born to us a year later. When Carol was three years old, in the spring of 1940, and I was expecting our second child in less than two months, the Lord made an extraordinary "invasion" into my life.

Nothing unusual had happened that particular day. It was just an ordinary day followed by what began as just another ordinary night. It turned out to be an unforgettable one, for in the middle of the night I had what must be called a vision. It was not a dream for I was not asleep and saw everything quite plainly.

In the vision I saw myself standing at the foot of a flight of steps going up on the outside of a limestone building to a second floor porch. At the same time I was standing there myself, looking at the unusual building. I was particularly impressed with the large, rectangular stones, each one directly on top of the other, because buildings made of such cut stones are unknown in Hawaii. I had never even seen a picture of one.

As I began to mount the stairs, an odd-looking, short, brown being confronted me and grabbed hold of me. It was very strong and tried to throw me down the stone steps. Desperately fighting my way to the top of the stairs, I somehow managed to knock the creature down so that it tumbled down the steps to the pavement below and lay still where it fell.

"There," I cried, "I killed you! I killed you!"

I stepped onto the porch which was walled on one side. On the other side the wall was low, about three feet high, and open the rest of the way up to the ceiling. Moving along the porch, a left turn took me into one end of a large long room with a stone floor. There was no furniture in the room. What light there was came in through the three open windows. A stone ledge under each window made a built-in seat.

There, on one of the window seats in a semi-reclining position was the Lord Jesus! I recognized Him immediately. He was leaning on one elbow, chin in hand, legs drawn up under Him. His only clothing was a short white garment around His loins. His dark hair reached to His shoulders.

Quickly I crossed the room to Him, knelt down, and looked into His brown eyes. They were simply pools of love, indescribable love, and compassion. Yet, I saw a kind of sadness in them, too. Oh, if only we could truly see and know the love of our Lord, we would never be the same!

"Oh, Jesus! Jesus," I exclaimed, "I killed him! Someone tried to kill me and I killed him!"

"I know, Irene, I know." The words were spoken evenly and reassuringly, the voice deep and full. "He tried to keep you from coming to Me. But nothing shall harm you. Nothing." There was a pause. "Now," He continued, "you must go. You will come to two roads where there is a fork in the road you are on. When you come to the fork you must choose which road to take. When you come to the end of it, you'll know if you have chosen the right one, for I shall be there to tell you."

In the next instant there I was, on the road which forked just ahead. Again, there was the strange sensation of being both participant and spectator at one and the same time, as I stood there at the fork in the road, while also seeing myself there in my pregnant condition.

Both roads looked long. The fork to my left was a wide road with lots of green grass and all kinds of beautiful roses alongside, including climbers and tree roses which I had never seen before. The fork to my right was a narrow road with some muddy places in it, some stony and uneven parts as well as some smooth stretches.

"Oh, that must be for the rich people," I said to myself, looking at the lovely wide road. "I'll take the other one for I am poor."

I set out on the narrow road, carefully picking my way over the muddy places and rough spots. The road went on and on and I was getting very tired.

Then I saw it—just ahead—a tiny, little unpainted church. I went up the three steps onto a small porch and looked inside the door. It was completely empty of furniture inside, but filled with a gloriously beautiful, bright golden light. I stood amazed for a moment, then slipped off my shoes, went inside, and sat down on the floor near the front of the room. From the front, off to the right and above me, came a great burst of blazingly bright, golden light, a shimmering sunburst radiating in all directions. It was many times more brilliant than the light already in the room.

All my weariness disappeared.

"Irene, you have chosen the right road." The voice was coming from out of that radiant light. I recognized the dear voice as the voice of Jesus I had heard earlier.

In the next instant I was back in my own bed. I sat bolt upright, shook Bill awake, and tried to tell him what had just happened. He didn't understand. How could he?

"It's just a crazy dream," he said. "Go back to sleep."

It was two o'clock in the morning, but sleep was impossible! I lay awake, again with that extraordinary warmth inside and a certain excitement pulsing through me such as I had experienced after hearing the heavenly music. This night's experience was too real to slough off as a crazy dream.

At breakfast time I again tried to tell Bill about it. Still unable to understand, he forbid me to speak of it to anyone lest they think I was insane. I could still see, I could still feel, the love in the eyes of Jesus. Bill left for work at the sugar mill where he was assistant sugar boiler.

It was about noon when I suddenly became very ill. The baby's position had shifted so that it was quite high under my ribs and I could hardly breathe. We didn't have a phone, so I could not call for help.

I stumbled outside where a neighbor woman saw me.

"Please, run quickly and call my husband," I gasped.

"You're going to have your baby?" she asked.

"No, it isn't time. It's something else. Please run," I pleaded. "Run quickly."

She ran and called Bill at the mill while I literally crawled up the steps into the house and into bed. My strength had drained away. I was losing all feeling and struggling for breath.

Bill called the doctor and raced home. When the doctor arrived he could see that there wasn't time to call an ambulance, so they rushed me to the hospital by car, sounding the horn all the way.

"Call the family. She's dying," the doctor told Bill bluntly. Bill immediately called my mother.

The doctor ordered something from a nurse, but she returned with the wrong thing. Consequently, I received no medication. Apparently, the baby's position had shifted to cause such pressure on the diaphragm that it could not function. I was literally suffocating to death and had turned blue all over. The doctor could only watch helplessly.

Suddenly, inexplicably, the baby dropped down and I began to breathe normally. My pulse, blood pressure, everything returned to normal. In a matter of minutes I felt fine.

In utter amazement the doctor cried out, "Oh, God! I'm seeing a miracle! Good Lord, I'm seeing a miracle!"

Aware that I had just been very close to death, I was reminded of the vision of the night before and started to say something.

"What did you say?" the doctor asked.

"Nothing," I said, remembering that Bill didn't want me to speak of it to anyone. I understood, somehow, that the struggle with the brown being on the stairs in the vision was the struggle with death I had just gone through.

A week later I was in the doctor's office for my next appointment. When the doctor heard my name called, he came out to the waiting room, greeted me, and put his arm around me as he presented me to everyone there.

"I want you to take a good look at this woman," he said, his gaze sweeping the faces of the waiting patients. "You are looking at a living miracle. Last week this woman had one foot in the grave and the other close behind. Now, as you can see, she is fine. Remember this and remember it well. She is a living miracle." Whether or not the patients were impressed, I don't know, but my doctor certainly was!

In response to Bill's phone call to my mother, she had come to Hilo. During her visit I told her about the vision I'd had.

Mother remonstrated rather emphatically, "Irene, married women cannot possibly see the Lord Jesus."

When Mother returned home to Kona, she told my grandmother about it. Grandmother, herself, came to Hilo to inquire about this "dream." I told her as well as I could.

"Well, you have sinned terribly," she told me firmly. "You married without your parents' consent. That is why you had such a dream, because married women do not dream of the Lord or see Him. You must ask the Lord to forgive you. Now, you go to church and you kneel down and ask God's forgiveness."

Neither Bill nor I attended church, but I did go, alone, the next Sunday. Both my mother and grandmother looked upon the experience I'd had as a shameful thing. Why, I don't know. It was as real as any life experience can be and it had touched me deeply.

At that time I knew nothing of the Scripture which says, "...broad is the way, that leadeth to destruction...and narrow is the way, which leadeth unto life" (Matt. 7:13,14). The two roads in the vision, one wide and one narrow, meant to me that the one I had chosen was not an easy road, but Jesus had assured me, "You have chosen the right road."

Neither did I know that Jesus had said, "I am the way, the truth, and the life" (John 14:6). Yet the Lord Himself was beginning to teach and lead me in His truth and His love even before I had His written Word.

What an encouragement it should be to you and me to realize that the Lord our God is quite able to reveal Himself to us, to instruct, guide, and comfort us apart from any human agency or printed word, if we should ever find ourselves without them.

The baby I was carrying, Joan Ellen, was born in due time, and in 1941 our third daughter, Diane, arrived to complete our family. It was many years later, in 1976, when the Lord "completed" the portion of the vision of the limestone building and the room in it which I had seen. But more about that later.

"Jesus saith unto him, 'I am the way, the truth, and the life: no man cometh unto the Father, but by me' " *(John 14:6).*

Irene Jenkins, 1933, twelve years old.

5

A BIBLE? WHAT'S THAT?

In 1943 Bill was transferred to Honolulu to work. Honolulu had been home for the first nine years of my life, so I welcomed the move. It was war time and housing was scarce. It took nearly a year for us to get settled into a satisfactory place to live.

Soon afterward, Carol, then seven years old, became ill. She had a fever which stubbornly refused to go down and she could not retain food or liquids of any kind. A friend of ours suggested that I take her to a Hawaiian lady she knew, whom I'll call Mrs. Pua, who probably could help Carol. So I arranged to take her.

Mrs. Pua was a kindly, soft-spoken, motherly person. She massaged Carol's abdomen, her hands moving gently but surely, while she prayed for her. She asked me to bring Carol back each of the next two days. When she had finished massaging and praying over Carol the third day, she sat back and looked inquiringly at me.

"Child, what is it about you? What do you have?" she asked.

"Why, nothing," I answered uncertainly.

"Yes, you do, for the Lord's Holy Spirit has shown me so."

Her question was unsettling because I felt it must have something to do with the vision I'd had. What would make her ask such a question? It made me uncomfortable and a little afraid of her.

"If you mean the 'dreams,' " I told her, "I am not to tell anyone about them because married women are not to dream about the Lord. Besides, people will think I am crazy."

"It's all right," Mrs. Pua assured me, "the Lord wants you to tell me."

So I told her about hearing the heavenly music, about seeing the limestone building, the two roads, everything. She listened attentively.

"Some day God is going to use you among our people," she said quietly.

What a strange thing for this woman to say. I did not understand what she meant and so felt even more afraid of her. Little did I know then that she was speaking prophetically.

Then she asked, "Irene, do you have a Bible?"

"A Bible? What is that?"

"The Word of God," she replied.

"What is that?" I asked again.

"Good Lord!" she exclaimed. "Don't you know? You sit right here. I'll be right back." With this Mrs. Pua disappeared into another room and returned with a black book in her hand.

"Here child, take this," she said, as she extended the book to me.

"Oh, I'm sorry, but I can't accept it," I protested. "I have no money to pay for it."

"I don't want any money for it. I just want you to take it."

"Oh," I said, brightening. "You're loaning me the book so I can read it and bring it back. All right."

"Child, you don't understand. I'm giving you the book. This is a Bible, God's Word, and the Lord wants me to give it to you. You are to take it and read it." Mrs. Pua pressed the book into my hands.

So, home I went with the book. Carol appeared to be fully recovered and after lunch, while the girls were taking their naps, I began thumbing through the pages of the black book called the Bible, starting at the beginning. Mrs. Pua had told me nothing about the book, not even mentioning that it was divided into the Old Testament and the New Testament. There were long, hard-to-pronounce names, lots of "begats," many things which had no meaning to me. With a shrug I closed the book, put it up on a closet shelf under my hat box and soon forgot about it.

However, I never forgot Mrs. Pua's words to me, "Some day God is going to use you among our people." Although I never saw her again, I learned, years later, that she was the wife of a Pentecostal minister. By that time I understood that God through the Holy Spirit had been showing her things about me.

God had used a problem situation—in this case, Carol's illness—to bring into my life something He knew I needed (the Bible), even though I failed to recognize it at the time. It was a valuable lesson, one I have had brought home to me many times: our problems may be God's opportunities.

"Every good giving and every perfect gift is from above..."
(James 1:17; lit.).

6

VISITS BY NIGHT

Visions, dreams, night visions—God has communicated to men by such means throughout biblical history from beginning to end. Why? Most any young mother could suggest one possible reason: the daily hubbub has subsided, all is quiet, even the mind is still and not full of busy thoughts, so God may be better able to get through! That seemed to be my experience as our Lord began revealing more of Himself and His Word to me.

In 1945, about five years after seeing Jesus in the limestone building, He appeared one night in a very vivid, clear vision. This time He was in the midst of a thick, shining white cloud, wearing a wine-red robe, but He was visible only from His waist up. He began speaking, first a personal word for me, then concluded with a simple command:

"Go and tell," He said firmly, then repeated the word, "Go and tell." As He receded in the vision I could still hear the words clearly, "Go and tell."

In the next instant I was in our own neighborhood talking to a woman with whom I had only a speaking acquaintance, describing to her what I had just seen. The vision ended at that point.

Morning came and with it such a sense of having **lived** the experience. Strange as it may sound, I could feel a literal warmth, the warmth of love deep inside.

"Oh, another one of those crazy dreams!" Bill exclaimed when I told him about it. He did not understand such things, nor did I, so that made two of us!

Bill left for work. I looked at the clock. It was too early to go calling, but I couldn't wait and crossed the court to the home of the neighbor woman I had talked to in the vision. I knocked on her kitchen door, then retreated a few steps, surprised at my boldness.

The door opened a few inches and her face appeared, "Yes?" she asked.

Words came tumbling out of my mouth, "Please don't think I'm crazy," I pleaded. "Forgive me for coming so early in the morning, but please don't think I'm crazy." I then proceeded to tell her of the vision I'd had of seeing Jesus, of His words, "Go and tell," and then seeing her and telling her about it. Oddly enough, as I began relating the vision to her, I began shaking uncontrollably from head to foot. How disconcerting, in fact, embarrassing! Hastily, I crossed my arms, holding them tight, trying to stop it, but it was impossible. Even my lips were quivering. The woman stood listening at the door, saying nothing until I finished.

The trembling stopped and that same lovely warmth went all through me. At the same time a complete calm came over me. The woman looked at me with a strange expression on her face, then cried out softly, "Oh, Father, forgive me. Please forgive me. I believe. I'm sorry, I do believe."

My eyes must have opened wide in astonishment. What she saw I'll never know, but this I know—whatever it was, the Father knew that it was much needed for the effect it would have on her heart. He loved her enough to show it to her by means of another person, a neighbor she barely knew and who understood nothing of what was happening at the time.

What a wise, loving heavenly Father we have. Don't be too surprised if or when He uses some unsuspecting person to speak very wonderfully to your heart. Or perhaps you will be the unknowing instrument God uses. Either way both of you will be blessed.

———

It was only a couple weeks after this incident that another, and very beautiful, vision of the night, or "dream" occurred...In it I was walking along a road amid open fields. Off to one side my attention was caught by the sight of a white dog and a white lamb romping playfully together. How unusual as dogs and sheep just do not play together. Both were so very white and clean, I stopped to marvel at them. What a sight! I had never seen such a thing before. It was beautiful.

As I watched the dog and the lamb, my attention was drawn to a low-lying mountain beyond them. A powerful glow of light had begun in the midst of it. It grew until it engulfed the mountain. Then, in the midst of the great glow of light, the Lord Jesus appeared standing with open arms, hands uplifted, clothed in a brilliant white, long-sleeved garment, with a round neckline, which reached to His ankles. His face and hair looked the same as when I had seen Him in the limestone building.

This time the light was so great it seemed to vibrate with a power that defies description. And it was so enormous, having grown larger than the mountain itself. It was awesome to behold, overwhelmingly awesome.

"Am I seeing God?" The cry came up from somewhere deep inside. "Am I seeing God?"

In answer, Jesus just extended His right hand to me. As He did I noticed a curious thing...His shadow was light, not dark as ours would be.

"Oh, how beautiful," I exclaimed aloud. "His shadow is light! He is light! He is all light! I reached out my hand to Him but He disappeared and I found myself back on the road and approaching the ocean.

As I looked out over the water, there was Jesus, standing on the waves and looking the same as before but this time wearing a wine-red robe. His feet were bare, His left hand outstretched. I extended my hand to Him and the "dream" ended. I was awake and greatly wondering about all that I had seen.

I wondered all the more after having a dream days later in which our Lord showed me many things with obvious symbolic meanings which I only vaguely understood. The more things I saw in these night-time experiences, the more questions I had. They created an insatiable hunger for answers and I began talking to the Lord about it.

"Lord, You're showing me many things I don't understand. Why? What do they mean? I must know," I told Him.

He said, "Go get the black book."

"The black book?"

"The black book you have under the hat box on the closet shelf. Go get the black book."

"Oh, the black book—the one Mrs. Pua gave me." I had almost forgotten about it.

I got the book down and began to read. This time I was so drawn to it I could hardly put it down. I hungrily read that Bible in every free moment I could find. When I could not understand it, which was most of the time, I would go to God and say, "Father, I don't understand this. I don't know what You are saying."

"Read it again," He would say.

How gracious and patient a teacher He is, and how loving. Slowly as I read I began to see that every one of the symbolic things I had seen in the dream was scriptural. What an encouragement that was. Not only had the Lord led me to read His Word, the Bible, to supply answers to my questions, but He also was assuring me that the dreams and visions He had given me were biblical—His Word to me in picture form.

Reading the Old Testament was slow going and took a long time, for I found much of it difficult to follow without the help of either a teacher or study guide. The New Testament was less difficult reading. During this period of reading through the Bible, the Lord continued to let me see things in dreams and visions which I would later come upon in my readings. For example, one time He showed me a single word, "WATCH," glowing in the heavens. How amazing then to find many places in the New Testament where Jesus admonishes us to "watch."

"Watch therefore: for ye know not what hour your Lord doth come" (Matt. 24:42).

"Watch ye therefore, and pray always, that ye may be accounted worthy to escape all these things that shall come to pass..." (Luke 21:36).

"And what I say unto you I say unto all, 'Watch' " (Mark 13:37).

Clearly, it seemed, we need to be alert and ready for Jesus' return, which could be at anytime, and not live carelessly or fail to pay attention to Him.

Another time the Lord showed me a short, golden sickle with a long handle in the heavens. It moved, ever so slowly, in a sweeping motion. I had never seen a sickle before. Later, in my reading, I came to some startling words: "And another angel came out of the temple, crying with a loud voice to him that sat on the cloud, 'Thrust in thy sickle, and reap: for the time is come for thee to reap; for the harvest of the earth is ripe.' And he that sat on the cloud thrust in his sickle on the earth; and the earth was reaped" (Rev. 14:15,16).

The next few verses describe an angel using another sickle for another harvest, one of God's wrath. It surely takes no special genius to understand that some day the time will be ripe for a glorious "harvest" when God gathers His own to Himself—those who keep His commandments and the faith of Jesus (see verse 12). The other, terrible harvest, will be of those who refuse to.

In another vision I saw a huge glass bottle of golden wheat on the floor of a barn. It was spinning like a top, the wheat threshing violently back and forth. Suddenly, the bottle overturned and the wheat spilled out on the floor. Words appeared on the wheat: "Keep holy the sabbath." It's hard to miss a message that is spelled out that plainly! In amazement I realized that the Lord was teaching me to set aside that one day for Him, keeping it as a holy day, as a day of rest, not a work day. At the time I had not yet read the Word which says, "Six days may work be done; but in the seventh is the sabbath of rest, holy to the Lord..." (Exod. 31:15).

Reading the Bible was beginning to change my life. How could I ever have thought it was just another book? Increasingly, it became my guiding light.

Certainly, my initial understandings of the visions and dreams were limited and I kept looking for fuller meanings of what the Lord was showing me. Occasionally, I would meet a minister and ask questions of him. My questioning was fruitless more often than not.

On one occasion a friend of ours brought her pastor and his wife to our home and asked me to share some of my experiences with them. I gladly did so, and they listened attentively. The pastor then stepped over to stand beside me and pray. After the prayer he put his Bible in my hands.

"Without looking, just open it," he said, "and put your finger on the page."

I did so. When we looked, my finger was pointing to Luke 16:22 which speaks of Lazarus, the beggar who had desired the rich man's crumbs, being carried by the angels to Abraham's bosom. In the context of the story Jesus was telling, the warning is plain: neither wealth nor position will count with God as proof of righteousness, of being right with Him.

The pastor spoke firmly, "Irene, the visions and dreams you have shared are from the Lord. He is teaching you."

The pastor's wife added, "As my husband was praying with you, I saw Jesus standing beside you."

What a welcome confirmation their words were! I now knew more surely that our Lord was, indeed, speaking to me. Although there was no further word of explanation and I never saw the couple again, I thank God for bringing them into my life and using them to strengthen me in Him.

Lord, I, too, would be used of You to encourage and strengthen the hearts of those who seek after You.

"Thou hast tried my heart; Thou hast visited me by night..." (Ps. 17:3; NASB).

7

SOME ROUGH PLACES

A long-time friend, whom I'll call Jean, (not her real name), had just arrived from Hilo with her young daughter to visit us in Honolulu for a few weeks during the summer vacation. After the initial flurry of greetings and a first get-acquainted look around, Jean and I sat down to relax and talk while our girls were busy playing.

Jean looked at me carefully. "There's something different about you, Irene," she said slowly. "You've changed."

I couldn't help smiling. "Yes, I suppose I have." And I began telling her about the unusual experiences I had been having. What a happy discovery to find that she, too, loved the Lord and was attending a Bible-believing church. When we knew each other in Hilo, I was aware that she went to church but we had never talked about Jesus. Now, as I shared what God had been doing in my life and shared His Word, we found ourselves talking of little else but Jesus the rest of that day and the days following.

Jean wanted to attend the church of her denomination while she was with us in Honolulu, so we went with her. At the church we met a family who invited us to their home for lunch, and we accepted the invitation.

While we were still at the table Jean exclaimed, "You should hear what Irene has to say about the Lord and how He has been dealing with her. When I knew her in Hilo she was not at all religious. Really, you must hear this!" So, again I shared.

When we went to church the next week, the same family urged us to have lunch with them again. They had invited others to come and hear me share about Jesus. It was the same story the third week although even more people were there, filling the living room to overflowing.

One young man who was there—I'll call him Len— listened very attentively. Later, after Jean had returned to Hilo, he came to visit us.

"Mrs. Lewers, would you be willing to come with me to a friend's home Friday evening and share your experiences?" he asked.

"Yes," I agreed, "if it's all right with my husband."

Bill answered carefully, "I can't say I understand all this, but if it is God I certainly don't want to be in the way."

Bill went with me that Friday evening. To our surprise a group of perhaps thirty people had gathered. When it was time for me to speak and I began sharing with them about Jesus, I began to tremble uncontrollably. Such trembling seemed to happen whenever I spoke of my experiences of the Lord. At the same time there would always be that gentle warmth flooding over and through me. The trembling in front of people was, frankly, a little disconcerting until I learned that it was a manifestation of the presence of God the Holy Spirit.

Little did I know this evening that, among those present, were some elders of the church—not until the following week when their pastor and his wife appeared at our door. I invited them in and he asked me to share with them, which I did.

At one point the pastor flatly said, "If you were being led of the Lord, you would not be eating meat." (They were vegetarians.)

"I believe everything has been given to us by God," I told him, "but I shall certainly ask the Lord about it."

In prayer I went to the Lord and inquired of Him, for with all my heart I believed His Word which says, "Ask, and it shall be given you; seek, and ye shall find; knock, and it shall be opened unto you" (Luke 11:9). So I asked the Lord to give me an answer when I opened the Bible.

The Bible opened to the fourth chapter of 1 Timothy where in verses 4 and 5 I read, "For every creature of God is good, and nothing is to be refused, if it be received with thanksgiving: for it is sanctified by the word of God and prayer." There was the answer! I thanked God for it.

True to his word, the pastor and his wife returned the following week. I was so glad to see them because I could tell them that God had indeed given me an answer. I showed them the passage of Scripture. I was quite taken aback by the pastor's reaction though, for he was very irate.

"Would you eat snake meat?" he demanded angrily.

"God has given us meat," I answered, "and when we pray and receive it with thanksgiving, His Word says that He will sanctify it."

Oh, my! How upset he was! His wife tried in vain to calm him. They left abruptly in a huff.

One afternoon, a few weeks later, his wife and he returned to our home bringing with them a woman who, they pointedly told me, was a doctor of theology. She allowed me no opportunity to talk. Sitting stiffly erect she said bluntly, "You are an angel of the devil and you had better rebuke these spirits." I was utterly dumbfounded and crushed. I sat there and wept openly.

"How," I asked between sobs, "can you condemn me when you have never heard me? The courts of our land allow even the worst criminal to speak for himself."

"I don't have to," she retorted. "Pastor has already told me all I need to hear."

I turned to the pastor. "Does this mean you could tell her, or anyone else, word for word exactly what I shared with you?"

He didn't answer at once, but looked down at the floor and finally answered, "No."

The theology doctor stood up abruptly. "You are truly of the devil," she said emphatically. And with that they left.

In tears, I hurried across the court to my Christian neighbor. Both her husband and she were supportive and comforting, assuring me that I was not of the devil. Their pastor understood that the Lord truly was teaching me. The husband was quite indignant and ready to go and speak to the doctor of theology and to the pastor.

"No," I said. "Jesus suffered abuse, why shouldn't I expect to if He did?"

It seemed as though the more I grew in the Lord, and shared the reality of His presence, the more opposition I experienced and the heavier the persecution became. Those with whom I shared would tell others who would sometimes come and ask why I had become so religious or so fanatic about Jesus. I would tell them how I had come to the Lord, how I had experienced His presence, how He was no further from us than they were from me.

Some would flatly tell me, "You're nuts," or, "You're crazy." A few people just listened without saying anything. Somewhat to my surprise, instead of feeling anger and resentment toward them, I found there was genuine love for them in my heart, but also a certain sadness. How sad it is that for so many people the concept of God is of some remote being far removed from where we are instead of the very near, loving Father I had come to know.

His presence was real, and His love. I felt it. Does anything else matter more than that?

"Blessed are ye, when men shall revile you, and persecute you, and shall say all manner of evil against you falsely, for my sake. Rejoice, and be exceeding glad: for great is your reward in heaven..." (Matt. 5:11,12).

8

THE LORD WHO HEALS

The doctor sitting across from me in his Honolulu office looked at me for a long moment before speaking.

"You have asked for the truth, Mrs. Lewers. The truth is that the inner ear infection, which you have, has no known cure at the present time and will be fatal to you. In the last stages there will be hemorrhaging that will take you quickly."

Slowly, his words sank in. Whatever else he said, probably including the medical terminology, was a blur. It's not easy to digest such news. And it must be very difficult for the doctor who gives it.

The news was not a total surprise. The problem had begun three years earlier, in 1944, when my ears began draining.

Gradually, the problem had worsened in spite of various doctors' efforts to treat it. My ear drums became so swollen, that when I spoke, the words would echo back in my head. Eventually my neck and throat became so swollen it was difficult to swallow. My head felt as though it had been stuffed with rags and my eyes often watered uncontrollably.

I thanked the doctor for telling me the truth. I reported to Bill what the doctor had said, all except about the hemorrhaging.

Meanwhile, I managed to continue doing my housework and caring for my husband and children.

In the summer of that year, 1947, the girls and I visited my parents in Kona for a month. While we were there the ear infection became acute, and they took me to their family doctor who gave me a careful examination.

"This is the same disease," he said, as he named the infection, "that took the life of your cousin when she was twelve years old. It is sure to take your life as well, for there is no known cure for it." He spoke gently, yet sadly.

What do you do when you know you have not long to live? How do you prepare for the inevitable?

One Sunday morning, my parents took a number of snapshots of me with my two younger brothers and two younger sisters. I understood what they were doing; they wanted each of the younger ones to have a picture with their older sister. For my parents it was a realistic preparation for what lay ahead. Part of my own preparation was asking my parent's forgiveness for any hurt I may have caused them and to express my forgiveness to them for whatever hurts they had caused me.

My ears got so bad, especially the right one, that I had to sleep sitting up. Through all the pain and fatigue I kept thinking of Jesus and of all He endured...the beating, mocking, spitting on, the scourging, and finally the terrible hanging on a cross. Looking on Him and all He endured for me, a sinner, made me keep still. In all of His terrible suffering He did not cry out or complain. My own pain seemed as nothing in comparison to His. By keeping my eyes on Jesus, focusing on Him, I could draw strength from Him. In a very real way He was my strength and my help. When the family doctor stopped by to see me each morning and evening, we would talk about Jesus.

Sometime during the third night of sitting up, I drifted off into a kind of half sleep and saw myself moving through an area of pitch blackness, a total darkness such as I had never seen. Yet, in it, I saw white forearms moving, as though swimming through the blackness. Then, in the distance, there appeared a great, golden, brilliant light and somehow I knew that, along with the others who must be around me, I was headed toward that light. A great joy welled up inside of me.

Then I heard my name called—three times—"Irene, Irene, Irene," and felt myself come back. Suddenly, my mother was there by my bed, bending over me, and her arms around me. She was trembling.

"Don't waken Sis, Mother," I said softly. "I know I am dying."

"Come, get up Irene. Let's go into the bathroom," she urged as she lifted my shoulders.

Mother helped me down the hall to the bathroom, closing the door behind us so we could speak without disturbing anyone. I told her what had just happened to me and she told me what had just happened to her. She had been asleep but wakened with a start and with the distinct impression that I was dying. She had gotten up and come running down the hall calling, "Irene, Irene, Irene."

I had heard her calling. So had the Lord and He had me come back. Mother knew then that the Lord was surely with me. The severity of the attack did ease. Perhaps the incident encouraged Mother for she soon began going to church again, to one my younger brothers and sisters liked. They all became active in it. My dad, too, sometimes participated.

After a month's stay with my parents, the girls and I returned home. No one had told Bill how ill I had been, for I had not wanted to worry him, so he was unprepared to greet such a painfully thin wife and registered shock when he saw me.

For awhile I was getting along, but took a turn for the worse in July, 1948 and started swelling outside. My earlobe was quite swollen, also the glands in my throat. Whenever I went outside, I covered my head with a long blue scarf so no one would see the cotton packing in my ears. There was a lot of drainage and the cotton had to be changed frequently. When it was wet, the buzzing in my ears worsened. Several different doctors prescribed various medications and treatments, including X-ray and ultra violet. Everything had been tried, but nothing had helped.

By now I had been walking with the Lord for three years. I had read of healings and believed with all my heart that nothing is impossible with God. Yet I did not ask Him to heal me, for I felt unworthy.

As the swelling increased, so did my concern for our children. Who would care for them when I was gone? My husband had no sisters and his mother had died when he was ten years old. My parents lived on another island and their youngest was only sixteen months older than our oldest daughter. Of their seven children, four were still very young. Bill could not expect my mother to care for our three girls.

There was nowhere to turn. I felt so alone and so sorry for my dear husband. I could see the weight of worry he was carrying, although he did not talk about it.

Finally, one Saturday night in August, I sat down with Carol Ann and told her that Jesus was going to take me home to be with Him. I told her that I loved her, her sisters, and her daddy very dearly. I explained to her that because her daddy was a young man, he would be needing the love and companionship of a wife after a while, and that he would need help with his girls. She was to learn to love whomever her daddy would choose to be their new mother and was to help her and help with her sisters. Wide-eyed, Carol listened, saying nothing. My heart was breaking, but there were no tears. I hugged her close and said, "I will always live in each of your hearts, even though you will not see me any more." Carol went to her bedroom and I to mine, there to weep softly, alone.

Sunday, Carol Ann stayed very close to me all day. We had visitors in the afternoon. I was ironing when they arrived, for I was trying to keep caught up with everything to ease things as much as possible when the Lord took me home. When the visitors left, I had finished the ironing and Bill went to check over the car. I was feeling so terribly sorry for Carol and regretted telling her what I had the day before. I encouraged her now to go out and play.

It's a curious trait of our human nature to take so many things for granted, not fully appreciating them until we are faced with the loss of them. Since being told I had not long to live, I became more keenly aware of the beauty all around me...of the flowers, trees, sky, the wind on my cheeks, appreciating them as never before, and thanking God for such things. My earthly treasures were my dear husband and my dear children. Who was going to take care of them?

Slipping into our bedroom, I fell on my knees and wept before the Lord. I regretted ironing clothes on the Lord's day. I poured out my heart to Him—all the hurt, loneliness, remorse, and despair— sobbing long and hard.

At length, I asked our Lord to please let me live, if it were His will, that I might raise my children. I would not ask for another day of life after our youngest daughter reached the age of fifteen. I would gladly serve Him the rest of my life and tell of Him to every one who would listen. I asked Him to help me fast for twelve hours at a time taking neither food nor water from midnight 'til noon for three days, beginning that night, and I thanked Him. As I rose up and began preparing dinner, all was peace in my heart, where aching despair had been only moments before.

That night, starting the fast, I was up the usual five or six times during the night to change the cotton in my ears. The next night, Monday night, I had fallen asleep soon after saying my prayers, got up at midnight and went back to bed.

At about two in the morning, I heard my name being called, "Irene, you will get well." The voice spoke these words three times, each time stronger than the last. The presence I felt was so strong, so real, that I reached out from where I was lying to touch the person who had spoken. Then I realized that it must be the Lord.

"Whatever are you doing?" My husband had roused from sleep. I told him a voice had spoken to me. I knew it was the Lord telling me I would get well.

Expectantly, I went to have a look at myself in the bathroom mirror. I was still swollen and draining as much as ever. I changed the cotton and returned to bed, thanking God and so full of joy that it was a wonder I was able to fall asleep again.

In the morning, at breakfast, I again told Bill what had happened. From the look on his face, he appeared to be more afraid for me than anything else. He left for work and the girls left for school.

My Christian friend came over that morning to see how things were going, for she was quite concerned about me. I told her how the Lord had spoken to me.

"That," she said emphatically, "was not the Lord. It if had been God, He would not tell you, 'You are going to get well.' He would have healed you right then. That," she said, "was the devil."

I was shocked! "No! It was the Lord," I said just as emphatically. "God would not allow Satan to do such a thing in my hour of great need. I know it was the Lord."

When she left, I ran into the bedroom, fell on my knees, and cried to the Lord. No one understood or even believed me. I thought I could understand a little of how Jesus must have felt in the Garden of Gethsemane when He sweat great drops of blood the night before He was crucified. However absurd it was to think of such a thing, I did, for at that point I was so crushed and felt so terribly alone it seemed unbearable. But the Lord understands and He is sufficient, an ever-present help.

From behind me I felt two strong arms gently lift me to my feet, and a warmth of love and peace came flooding over me. The tears stopped and joy welled up instead. I knew then beyond the slightest doubt that I was healed although there still was no visible evidence of it.

Bill came home at lunch time to check on me and was still quite worried when he returned to work. He found me still full of joy when he got home that evening.

That night I did not get up even once to change the cotton packs in my ears. I actually slept all night for the first time in over two years. When I got up the next morning, there was no swelling, no drainage, and no pain. God had wonderfully, completely healed me!

In the words of the apostle Peter, I did indeed "...rejoice with joy unspeakable and full of glory" (1 Pet. 1:8), filled with such awe and gratitude, such love and peace, there were no words to express them. All I could do was to humbly thank God for His love and mercy. When the Great Physician heals, it is a gracious gift of love, freely given, although very costly. But He never sends a bill, for He, Himself, paid the price in full on Calvary's cross.

The only remnant of the disease, and one which I still have, is some scar tissue in one ear that was caused by a medication that one doctor prescribed. When I told our doctor what had happened and he saw for himself that I was well, he was dumbfounded.

"I've heard of things like this," he said, "but this is the first time I have seen such a thing."

Different people had different reactions when I told them how God had healed me, some of whom knew how very ill I had been. Some just listened, some did not believe me. One actually asked if I was a witch because I had been healed! In Hawaii at that time we did not know about the power of God to heal apart from medical treatment.

Bill didn't know what to make of it, but the girls and he were very thankful to have me well. Bill was, in fact, quite moved by this miracle of God's healing and began to believe and open his heart to God and His Word from that time on.

God has declared, "I am the Lord that healeth thee" (Exod. 15:26). God does not change. He is "...the same yesterday, and today, and forever'' (Heb. 13:8; NIV). Yet I do not find Him explaining the whys, the hows, and the whens of His healing power. The man blind from birth, whom Jesus healed, had no explanations, but simply said, ''...whereas I was blind, now I see'' (John 9:25). Likewise, I can only say in praise to God, ''Whereas I was sick unto death, now I am healed.'' Since that day I have both seen and heard of countless proven instances of God's grace and power to heal all kinds of physical and spiritual problems. Our God is so great that, as Jesus said, ''...with God all things are possible'' (Mark 10:27). To deny the power of God to heal apart from medical or other professional treatment is to deny the power of God, period. It is unbelief.

When the father of the epileptic boy brought him to Jesus, he was not sure Jesus could or would help them. Hear our Lord's reply: ''If thou canst believe, all things are possible to him that believeth'' (Mark 9:23). Then hear the father's tearful response as he cried out, ''Lord, I believe; help thou mine unbelief'' (Mark 9:24). If doubts creep in, let that be your heart cry and mine, for God will honor it. Jesus had compassion on that boy and healed him (Mark 9:25). Jesus had compassion on me and healed me. Praise His name!

> *"The cords of the grave coiled around me; the snares of death confronted me. In my distress I called to the Lord; I cried to my God for help...He reached down from on high and took hold of me; he drew me out of deep waters"* (Ps. 18:5,6,16; NIV).

A POSTSCRIPT

During the last two years of the ear problem I used a long blue scarf over my head to conceal the cotton in my ears. Carol Ann liked it so much that she said all she wanted for Christmas was a picture of me wearing that scarf. In front of the camera at the photographer's studio, the photographer first asked me to think of my husband, then anything I wished. At once I thought of Jesus.

''I should not have seen that,'' he said, after snapping the picture.

Puzzled, I asked, ''What do you mean? What did you see?''

He only walked away without answering. He was even unwilling for me to see the proof of that particular pose when I returned for them. When I took the proofs home, it was that pose which Carol chose for her Christmas present.

I was unprepared for the comments and jokes friends would make when they saw it. They would kiddingly ask me if I was trying to copy the blessed Mother Mary in the picture. I only replied, "I could hardly copy someone that I have never seen."

The ribbing continued when we moved to the mainland. One evening we were speaking of the Lord with a group of people in our home. I was asked why I had such faith in the Lord. I shared with them the miraculous healing of my ears and my husband brought out the picture to show them. The following day a member of the group called to say that one of them had been very upset by the picture. She felt I was trying to imitate the blessed Mother, a sacrilege which angered her. She called me a hypocrite.

Puzzled, I prayed about it and then went to a prayer-and-share meeting. At one point the pastor called forward any who needed healing. As he prayed for them, I, too, was praying when the Holy Spirit spoke to my heart saying, "Open your eyes and look." As I opened my eyes, I noticed a particular look on the faces of some of the women there that was the same as the one in the picture.

As soon as I got home I called the woman who had informed me of the meeting. I told her what I had seen and asked her to come, too. She did the very next week and she saw the same look on certain faces that I had seen. She was deeply moved. It was now 1973; the picture was taken in 1946. We were seeing an identical look in the picture and on certain faces of Christians in prayer many years and hundreds of miles apart. We began to see that God the Holy Spirit is literally timeless and unchanging as He is reflected in the very faces of God's children.

The picture will always be a visual reminder to me of God's mercy and grace, His loving kindness to me in giving me another chance to live the rest of my life serving Him.

> *"Great is Thy faithfulness; great is Thy faithfulness.*
> *Morning by morning new mercies I see.*
> *All I have needed Thy hand hast provided.*
> *Great is Thy faithfulness, Lord, unto me."*

(Copyright 1923, 1951, Hope Publishing Company).

9

A LIGHT, LOVE, AND A LESSON

Picture postcards of Hawaii invariably show it bathed in sunshine, but there's plenty of rain there, too. Tropical rainstorms, often with thunder and lightning, are common and when it rains, it can really pour!

It was on such a day that I was in the kitchen mixing up a cake while the children were down for naps. Singing to the Lord as I worked, I was vigorously creaming together the shortening and the sugar when I became aware of a big splotch of bright light on the wall to my left.

"Now that's odd," I thought aloud. "If the sun were shining I would think it was hitting a piece of glass or a mirror somewhere. But it's raining. It's raining hard." Fascinated, I stared at that glowing light for several moments.

"Lord Jesus, is that You?" I asked wonderingly.

Immediately, I felt the gentle embrace of arms encircling me from behind. In that moment such an overwhelming love enveloped and filled my being, such great joy welled up inside, that it could not be contained and I began singing as I had never sung before. My voice went soaring into a higher range than had ever before been within my reach, nor has it been since.

Jesus once said, "He that hath My commandments and keepeth them, he it is that loveth Me, and he that loveth Me shall be loved of My Father and I will love him and will **manifest Myself** to him" (John 14:21). What a promise! Yes, He does manifest His presence and He does so in many ways. Since "God is light," (1 John 1:5) and "God is love," (1 John 4:16) it should not be too surprising if He chooses to manifest His presence as light and love.

"This love and joy you're telling me about—can you explain a little more?" Bill was trying to understand when I described to him what had happened.

What words could I use? What could I say except that it was, as Peter said, "unspeakable"—inexpressible—and like nothing I had ever before experienced. Bill said nothing more. How difficult it must have been for him, as a husband who loved his wife, to have her trying to describe a love and joy that so greatly surpassed what he could give her.

Bill was aware that I was changing in a number of ways. For one thing, I was becoming far more patient than I used to be. When I made mistakes I would ask forgiveness and go on.

It is Bill's nature to be protective and temperamental. It was hard on him when people treated me rudely. Their verbal attacks had embarrassed, humiliated, and angered him. Imagine, if you will, what it is like to be told that your wife is crazy, that she should have her head examined. That hurts. On occasion he would be upset with me, too, because I would apologize to the other person even when, as Bill knew, I was in the right.

"Why do you make yourself a doormat and let them walk all over you?" he would ask indignantly.

"Honey," I would say, "they don't understand because they don't really know the Lord; they're not living in a close, personal relationship with Him." Even though they went to church and we did not, (simply because we didn't know where to go), I knew that I **knew** Jesus. Daily I was seeking a closer walk with Him. I read my Bible and prayed. I prayed for my family and for my people in Hawaii. My heart ached for them to know Jesus.

One evening, a couple who were friends of ours stopped by. The husband was a Jew and a firm disbeliever in Jesus. The wife was a Gentile who had professed her belief in God and in Jesus Christ. From time to time we had talked about Jesus. This particular evening they brought a young Jewish man with them. He was full of questions.

In the course of our conversation that evening in early 1947, I spoke of Jesus as being the Messiah and of His love for His chosen people, the Jews.

"One day soon they will return to the Holy Land, to Israel," I said.

"When that happens, It will be as though Jesus' hand is on the door, ready to open it as soon as He hears His Father say, 'It is finished.' Jesus will then return to gather His body, the Church, to Himself."

The disbelieving husband swung on me saying, "What you need is a psychiatrist." Turning to my husband, he added, "Bill, you'd better take her to one." (Small wonder that Bill was very upset when they left.)

Nor was it easy for me, for not only was he rude to me but he was very crude and unkind to his wife. It would pain me deeply when he spoke to her in a crass, uncaring way, making unreasonable demands in an overbearing manner. I would think, "Why can't he just leave her alone, or keel over, or something?"

After one such display of ill-temper in our presence, I allowed myself to become very upset, to the point of hating the man. I was still "stirred up" when I went to bed that night. During the night I got up and from out of nowhere a terrible fear came over me. It made no sense. What was there to fear? Yet it was so awful that I almost ran back to bed. Being close to my husband should have reassured me, but instead, the fear grew worse. Silently, I cried out to God for help. God is always faithful to hear a heart-cry and in His faithfulness He showed me the problem: there was sin in my heart because I had judged a man and even wished him dead. How awful! What had disturbed me so much was none of my business; it was theirs.

In repentance I asked the Lord for forgiveness and for His help to never make such a mistake again. God is faithful and just to forgive every repentant heart and He forgave me right then and there. It is in repentance that the soul is cleansed and fellowship with God is restored. The awareness of His forgiveness was followed by such a strong sense of the nearness of His presence that I actually reached out to touch Him.

The lesson I learned that night has been an invaluable one. After that it was easier to hear problems without resentment toward anyone and to point them to Jesus.

In May of 1948 Israel was restored as a nation to the Jews. One morning, a couple of months later, the phone rang. It was the young Jew who had been so full of questions the evening our friends had brought him to our home.

"Mrs. Lewers, do you remember the evening when I was in your home and you talked about Jesus and about the Jews and about the Holy Land being returned to them as a nation?"

"Yes," I replied. "I remember."

"Please," he said earnestly, "please tell me the name of the book you got that from. I must read it. I have not been able to forget what you said ever since Israel has been restored as a nation. Now I know that Jesus must be the Messiah!"

Oh, how glad I was to be able to tell him that the book he wanted to read was the Holy Bible! I fully expect to meet that young man in heaven some day.

"The entrance of Thy words giveth light; it giveth understanding unto the simple" *(Ps. 119:130).*

10

THE LORD WHO LEADS

With World War II ended, we started looking for a home to buy or property on which to build. We began a careful search. In prayer, I asked the Lord to lead us, to show us where He wanted us to live, for our home was to be His. I asked Him for a sign. I asked for a holly berry tree to be on the property. (The holly berry tree is not commonly found in Hawaii.)

One evening we noticed an ad for a lot in Alewa Heights in Honolulu. Arrangements were made for the realtor to show me the lot. A friend accompanied me when I went to see it. My attention was first drawn to a beautiful home across the street.

Just then I heard my friend cry out, "Irene, look—your holly berry tree," and then she counted seven of them! Excitedly, she told the realtor all about my petition.

"It's their land," she said. "She has asked the Lord to show her where He wants them to live, and to give her a holly berry tree for a sign."

The realtor was visibly shaken. "The asking price is $7,500," he informed us. That was a lot of money to pay for a lot in those days.

"We'll give them $5,000 for it and not a penny more," I told him, "because that is the amount I feel we are supposed to pay."

"They'll never let it go for that," he warned. "This property is fee simple land. It has to be bought outright, not like so much of the property in Oahu which is lease land."

I said, "The offer stands—not a penny more."

My friend spoke up and said to him, "You might as well deliver the offer, because the Lord has shown her that this is to be their property. You'll see."

Back at home I called my husband and told him of the morning's events. He agreed to look at the lot with me when he came home from work. Early that afternoon the realtor called. He had spoken to the owners of the lot and submitted our offer to them. He was incredulous when they agreed to accept our "$5,000 and not a penny more."

That evening when we went to look at the lot, my husband stood and looked in amazement at the seven holly berry trees. The lot commanded a magnificent view of Honolulu and the sparkling blue waters of the Pacific Ocean. Best of all, we knew this was God's doing.

We saw God's hand moving in many ways as we proceeded with the building of our home in that year of 1948. Although we were advised to get bids from three contractors, the Lord showed me which contractor to hire without a bid. At that time it was taking three to four months to arrange for a loan; ours took only three days. Our contractor had all the lumber he needed, so the longshoremen's strike that was on did not affect us. He did extra things for us at no extra cost to us, such as building cabinets in the bathroom and loaning us his truck to haul dirt to fill in the front yard to make it level with the road. He was a Buddhist, but God was touching his heart.

One day we were sitting at the kitchen table discussing the building. I thanked him for his patience with us and our many questions. He asked then why I was different from most people. The only answer to that question is Jesus and so I shared Jesus with him. He kept asking questions which I answered as the Holy Spirit led me. Finally, I asked him if he would like to ask Jesus into his own heart.

"No, not now," was his reply. "I'm too busy for this Jesus now. When I'm old I'll look for you and then I'll ask this Jesus into my heart."

"That my be too late," I protested. "You could be killed in an accident or die of a heart attack and there would be no more time for you."

"No," he said, "I'll wait."

He waited and waited. More than twenty years passed before he did indeed die of a heart attack. When I had occasion to see his wife some time later, I learned that he had talked about me but had not accepted the Lord before he died. My heart nearly broke. I prayed, "How many, O Lord, will be lost, never able to enter the kingdom of God because they chose to wait?" What a terrible price to pay for more time in this fallen world, in Satan's playground. How tragic.

When we start walking with Jesus and learn to know Him, our lives will be filled with a joy and a peace that we have not known before. This is not to say that problems will disappear; we'll still have problems, but we will have Jesus. He doesn't have problems—only plans and provision for them. His grace is available to us, His enablement, and we'll know His joy and His peace that exceeds the limits of our understanding. We'll be living in that place where we can praise Him in all things, for He is faithful. Halleluia!

Not a single one of us can know with any certainty what even the next minute holds for us. Our lives can be snuffed out as quickly and unexpectedly as a candle flame. Not one person reading these words needs to wait another minute if he has not accepted the Lord Jesus Christ into his heart. Please—don't wait. Admit to Him that you are a sinner, that you have fallen short of His just commands, that He took your place and died for your sins and that He rose again that you might have eternal life now. Yield your life to Him and trust Him, thanking Him for His mercy and grace to you. Believe that by the Holy Spirit, He is living in the innermost part of your being and you now are truly a son or daughter of God the Father.

"Make me know Thy ways, O Lord; teach me Thy paths. Lead me in Thy truth and teach me, for Thou art the God of my salvation" (Ps. 25:4,5; NASB).

11

ALOHA HAWAII

We moved into our new home in March of 1949 with more than the usual joy for we were so aware of God's hand of blessing upon it. He plainly had chosen the site and made all sorts of provision during the building. We worked hard inside and out, Bill himself finishing off the full basement.

"Lord, bless this home and all who enter it with Your peace and love. And help us, Lord, to be good and faithful caretakers of it." Such was my earnest prayer.

Alewa Heights is a mountainous area above Honolulu. From where our house was situated high upon the side of a hill, we could see much of the city spread out below us. Often, as I looked out of our big picture window, I couldn't help wondering how many of all those people down there truly knew the Lord Jesus.

One morning the Lord gave me a short but vivid vision. In it I was looking out over the city when I saw a huge tidal wave come up out of the ocean. It crashed upon the land, smashing everything in its path till it reached the foot of the hill where we lived. As I watched, the water receded. To my horror I saw no homes, no buildings, nothing left standing where the wave had hit. It was a terrible sight.

"Oh, God, have mercy!" I cried out.

The vision had moved me deeply and disturbed me for some time. In time the Lord showed me that Hawaii would be filled with a great many people following destructive, sin-filled ways. Sin, the occult, superstition (what we call old Hawaiiana) would sweep over the islands like a mighty tidal wave. As a consequence and because of much apathy, many souls would be lost. I began to be burdened in my heart for our people.

There has always been a tendency for our island people, like so many others, to mix their pagan beliefs and fears with Christian belief. I think of a man carrying a suitcase full of pagan beliefs. When he sees a suitcase of what is called Christian belief, he decides he'd like that too, so he picks it up and adds it to the other one. He is then carrying two suitcases. He has not understood what true Christianity is. Anyone who would be a Christian must understand that the first suitcase with **all** its contents has to be completely abandoned.

It will never do to carry two suitcases. Jesus called it serving two masters. Inevitably, "...he will hate the one and love the other; or else he will hold to the one and despise the other" (Matt.6:24). Only those who love and serve God wholeheartedly will be prepared to spend eternity with Him.

How I love these dear people of mine. I am one of them. I feel for them and with them and thank God for having been born in Hawaii. My mother's parents were Europeans who were only children when they arrived in Kona. Hawaii's last king and queen were reigning then and my mother was born there. My dad was born in Missouri and landed in Honolulu while in the army before World War I. There he met and married my mother and there the first five of their children were born; the last two were born in Kona. My husband and our three daughters were all born in Hilo. We are grateful for our Hawaiian heritage. The friendliness of the island-born people is genuine. They are a warmly affectionate and gracious people who love music. Their warm "Aloha" (love) is typical of them and unforgettable. As it is in families, so it is with them—they may have their problems, but are quick to rally to the aid of one of their own if he needs help.

"But my people hath become lost sheep; their shepherds have caused them to go astray" (Jer. 50:6). Oh my people, how I long for you to earnestly seek the Lord our God and come to Jesus while there is still a little time. There is no other way to truth and life. No halfhearted commitment will do, for Jesus warns us, "Thus because you are lukewarm, and neither cold nor hot, I am about to spew you out of my mouth" (Rev. 3:16). We must take care that we are not just "playing church," following mere forms without substance.

In spite of criticism and other hindrances, I continued to share Jesus. Only God's grace kept me from being offended. He helped me understand that people who opposed me did not realize that they were actually coming against Him and that I should love them and pray for them. There were times, though, when I wept with longing and asked the Lord for a "family," for people who knew and loved Jesus as I did, people who would understand when I shared with them and they with me.

Looking back, I can see that many times I either came on too strong or tried to share more than people were able to receive. I pray they will forgive my overzealousness. Sometimes a new Christian is more like a bull in a china shop than a lamb in a meadow. Mistakes go with learning. However, our Father is wonderfully patient; He keeps loving us through our mistakes and, wonder of wonders, often redeems them!

In 1952 our Lord led me to start visiting a territorial hospital to sing and read the Bible to the patients. Thus began a long period of training and preparation for later ministry. Do you know what it is like to walk about in an ocean of love? I learned that at the hospital. What I had to give these lonely people was so little compared with what I received from them so abundantly. They were a source of much blessing and encouragement. Have you discovered that God's economy works that way?...that it's in giving that we receive?...that he who sows even a little in love will reap much more?

There were some sad farewells one May day in 1954, for it was my last visit with these dear people before leaving sunny Hawaii and moving to sunny California an ocean away, as the Lord was leading us.

Aloha, Hawaii! Hello, California!

"And lo, I am with you alway, even unto the end of the world" (Matt. 28:20).

———

12

I STAND AT THE DOOR

We did not feel we were total strangers when we arrived in California. My sister Alice and her husband were already here and had written about such phenomena as trees that lose all their leaves in winter. We were not prepared, though, for the vastness of this great land and its rich beauty. We first settled in San Mateo, near San Francisco. Then about five years later we moved to Campbell, which is at the south end of the San Francisco Bay, adjacent to San Jose.

The Lord continued to teach me through the Scriptures as well as through dreams and visions. It was in a dream in 1956 that I saw a certain winter scene so clearly. There was a small white stucco church nestled among tall, snow-laden pines. The figures of two persons were standing just outside the building. I recognized both persons as being Jesus, one as a grown man, the other as a boy of about twelve. Both were clothed in long, white garments. There was deep snow on the ground and it pained me to see our Lord outside in the cold and snow. I wondered, "Why isn't He inside?" The white garment He was wearing impressed me, for it was far whiter than the snow.

When I awoke I asked the Lord about it. "Why were You outside the church? And why did I see You also as a boy?''

No answer came. Was He unwilling to answer? No, when we ask, He will answer but He will do so in His way and in His time. I did mention the dream to Bill and a couple of others, then I forgot about it.

Six years passed. Bill and I were on a winter trip in the northern part of California. As we were driving along a mountain highway one Sunday morning we passed a church just off the road in a lovely wooded setting of tall pines. We pulled off onto the side road, stopped, and stepped out into the knee-deep snow. As I looked at the little church there was a quickening in my spirit.

''Bill, I've seen this church before.''

''How could you have seen this church before? You have never been here before.'' Of course, he was speaking what I very well knew. Then I remembered the dream of 1956. I was looking at the same church building I had seen in that dream! Now, in a sudden flash of insight, the understanding came that this particular church was one which represented many congregations. Recalling the two figures I had seen in the dream, I suddenly understood that seeing Jesus as a boy meant that even though these congregations were well established as to their building, they were immature and childish in their understanding of Him. Seeing Jesus as a man outside the church indicated that many had an intellectual ''head'' knowledge of Him and were involved in all kinds of activities and programs. Yet they lacked a true relationship with, and, a heart knowledge of Jesus Himself.

The message was loud and clear, a word to all of us; the real, the true Jesus, was and is still waiting out in the cold, outside the door of many hearts who are so busy doing their own good things that they never think of inviting Him in.

How many will be crying out, ''Lord, Lord,'' when Jesus comes, and be stunned to hear Him say, ''I never knew you (acknowledged you). Depart from me, you who practice lawlessness'' (Matt. 7:23; NASB).

Do you know the Lord? That is a very important question. Even more importantly, does the Lord know you? You and I had better be sure we can answer, ''yes,'' to both questions.

"Behold I stand at the door and knock; if anyone hears My voice and opens the door, I will come in to him and will dine with him and he with me" (Rev. 3:20; NASB).

Irene Lewers, age twenty-five.

13

PART OF THE FAMILY

In San Jose I was prompted to start ministering again in convalescent hospitals. The need and potential blessing was no less in California than in Hawaii. As this work got under way I was inspired to start the Aloha Choir to sing in the convalescent homes. By this time (1961) I had matured somewhat as a Christian and did not "come on" so strongly when I talked of Jesus. I was learning to simply love and to try to live in Christ-likeness. When I made mistakes, I repented and went on. The beautiful and faithful people in these places have been such a blessing to us who have gone to them. The Lord has forged a great bond of love between us. Some of them allowed me to share Jesus' word with them. The Aloha Choir continued for eight years.

In 1971, while training a new volunteer for work in a convalescent hospital near her home, I said to her, "Dear, you are ready now to go to the home and start working there. In time you will develop your own routines. Just pray and ask the Lord to guide you."

In tears she protested, "No, I don't want to go, not without you."

"All right I'll go with you the first time," I assured her.

"No," she said, "You don't understand. I don't want to leave

---

you. I don't have what you have and I want it.''

"What do I have that you want?'' I asked, perplexed.

"I don't know how to say it. There is something you have deep inside that I want to have too.''

"Oh,'' I said, "that is Jesus. Only He can give Himself to you, and He will. You have only to ask.''

"How?'' she pleaded, tears now streaming down her cheeks.

With the Lord's help, I explained from the Word of God. There was a hunger in her heart for God's Word and she asked me to please teach her.

"The Holy Spirit is the One who teaches,'' I explained, "but we could meet together and pray and seek the Lord and He will teach both of us.''

She came the following Tuesday evening—with five other people! With Bill and me there were eight of us. The Spirit of the Lord moved among us that evening as we gathered together around the Word. We read, we discussed, we shared, we learned and we grew as the group continued to meet each Tuesday.

One Tuesday evening in April of 1972, a woman came to the door and said, "I'm told you have a Bible class here. May I join you?'' We welcomed her.

As the evening progressed, she would look at me in wonderment and say, "You talk just like a pastor I know. You even act the same way he does and the people who go to that church. You are like them.''

After about the seventh or eighth time, I asked her, "Where is this church you're talking about?''

When she told me, she said she had been going to what they called "Prayer and Share'' on Wednesday mornings for over four months. "It's at ten o'clock tomorrow morning,'' she told me, and gave me the directions.

She had really piqued my curiosity, so I decided to go and see for myself. Following her directions, I found my way to the church and slipped into a pew just four rows from the front, right in the center in front of the platform. I was determined to be very careful and see if this pastor was truly a man led of the Lord. I watched everyone. The pastor came in and began leading the singing—with his eyes closed! I was not about to close my eyes, and watched him closely. Every time he opened his eyes there I was, staring at him.

After a while, the Lord spoke to my heart, saying, "Irene, I have now given you a family, a people like yourself." Softly, I wept, my heart overflowing. God is so faithful.

That evening I met my husband at the door when he came home from work. "You must come and see these people," I told him excitedly. "They're like me. I'm not some crazy fanatic or misfit." It is hard to express the relief and the release which that realization brought to me.

As Bill and I began to attend this church, God began to bring understanding of many things. For example, back in 1950 I'd had a short yet vivid early morning dream in which I saw in the heavens a group of people singing together. They appeared to be present day people dressed in present day street clothes, but I could not understand any of the words they were singing. When I got up that morning, I kept remembering how sweet their singing had sounded, yet in a strange language. I mentioned this to a number of people, puzzling over it.

Then in 1972 while attending my first charismatic meeting in our new home church, the Spirit of God fell over the congregation in such power that everyone began to sing in the Spirit, in words which were different from English. With uplifted faces their voices swelled together as one, then receded and swelled again, wave upon wave. I bowed my head in reverent awe, hands folded across my breast. Some words of Paul came to mind: "…making melody in your hearts to the Lord" (Eph. 5:19), and I realized that is what I was hearing. Then the Lord brought the dream back to me saying, "This is what I was showing you." I literally gasped in sheer amazement, tears streaming down my cheeks. The more I get to know the Lord, the more I am in awe of His greatness, His goodness, His beauty, His love, and His wonder-working ways. In today's vernacular, He "blows my mind" at times.

For the first time I began learning some of the terminology for what the Lord had been teaching me over the years. For example, I used to say that my heart burns and I am weeping inside. One day after the pastor had spoken of "carrying a burden," I asked him, "Is that when you heart weeps and burns?" He assured me that it was. Now I knew what to call it—there was a word for it—and I would understand others when they used the term.

I learned the meanings of words that helped my understanding. My first introduction to the word "grace" had been in asking God's blessing on our food at mealtime. How good to understand that God's grace means His unearned, unmerited favor. God's grace is given freely and richly.

Some things had to be "unlearned." When my ear disease was so bad in 1948 I had prayed, "Lord, please let me live until my youngest daughter is fifteen and I'll not ask You for another day of life after that." I didn't ask Him to heal me but to help me, which He did faithfully. Having given my word to Him, I felt unworthy to ask for any healing now. Foolish? Yes, terribly foolish. I had put myself under bondage to my own words. In our new church home I soon learned how wrong I was. I repented of my words and was set free, thank God. In Jesus we are free to come before the very throne of God and "...with thanksgiving let your requests be made known to Him" (Phil. 4:6).

As we continued to attend this church, Bill was drawn more and more to Jesus and in 1974 opened his heart to receive Him personally as Saviour and Lord. God had a new son.

Let me encourage the many women who have dear husbands in a situation much like Bill had been for so long. We wives are called to live Christ-like lives in our homes, that our husbands might see Jesus in us. The change must come in us first. Our first ministry is in our home to our husbands and family.

I learned not to preach to Bill but to love him in a fuller way. Sometimes I failed and became over-anxious. I had to learn that the calling of a soul to come to the Lord Jesus is the Holy Spirit's job, not mine. When I got in the way Bill was hindered. There are times when we are to share, times to love, times to encourage, to just be there—and at all times to pray!

Imagine hearing your husband one day saying in a public meeting, "I thank God for my wife's example over the years. It was by God's love flowing through her that I grew in my commitment to Jesus." Such was Bill's testimony as my heart overflowed in gratitude and praise to our Lord. As my husband and the head of the household, Bill is my spiritual covering, "my protective umbrella," as we travel both near and far to share Jesus as the Holy Spirit directs. What a blessed privilege that is!

"For this cause I bow my knees unto the Father of our Lord Jesus Christ, of whom the whole family in heaven and earth is named" *(Eph. 3:14,15).*

14

GO...AND TELL...

Soon after finding a church family, I received three letters within three days from back home, one from Kona and two from Honolulu. I learned that a men's Christian fellowship group had made a trip to Honolulu as well as to Hilo and Kona where they ministered and shared the Lord. These men were reported to be on fire for the Lord.

While in Kona, one of the men in the group was sharing with a woman who knew me quite well.

"You talk just like Irene Lewers," she told him. "People here thought she was crazy."

"I would like to meet her," he said after they had talked a little more. "Where is she?"

"She now lives in California."

"By all means get her back here. Write and ask her to come back," he advised her. She followed his advice and wrote.

Then in Honolulu a friend of ours, out on her lunch hour, walked into a curio shop just to look around. She spotted a tiny book titled *Four Steps to Christ*, and asked the proprietress about it. The woman began to share Jesus with her.

"I'm out of time, but I'll be back tomorrow on my lunch hour," our friend told her. "You sound like a friend of mine who used to live here. People thought she was just too religious."

"True to her word, she returned the next day and the two women talked further. "Write to this friend of yours," the shop owner urged. "Ask her to come back."

The letter that came brought tears to my eyes. In it our friend said, "Come home, Irene, and tell us again what you told us before about Jesus, because you are one of us. You belong to us."

The third letter also mentioned the Christian fellowship men who talked about the Lord as much as I had and asked me to return. In seeking the Lord about this, He showed me that, yes, I was to go back and minister in Hawaii. I, of course, shared all this with Bill.

My husband's response was, "I don't understand all of this, but I don't intend to oppose God by saying, no you can't go."

About a week before I was to leave for Hawaii, I was busy cleaning the house on a Friday morning, singing to the Lord as I worked. Unexpectedly, He spoke to my heart saying, "Irene you are to go to the phone and call Pastor Fry's office, for you are going in to talk with him today."

"Yes, Lord," I answered, as I dropped everything and called the church office.

"What did you want to talk to Pastor about?" his secretary asked.

My reply must have made her wonder about the person at the other end of the line. "The Lord just now told me to call because He said I was going to talk with Pastor today."

"Well," she said after a moment, "someone just canceled a fifteen-minute appointment for three o'clock."

Praise the Lord. He had it all arranged. As I met with Pastor Fry at the appointed time, he asked, "What is it you have to tell me?" I told him how the Lord had sent me to him that afternoon.

"Is there something you are to do?" he asked, being very perceptive.

"Oh, yes. The Lord is sending me back to Hawaii," I said, pulling out the three letters to share with him.

"How long have you been a Christian?" was his next question.

"Since 1945." I then told him about the heavenly music in 1932 and the night vision in 1940, of the stone building in which I saw Jesus, and of the two roads. He listened carefully, then prayed with me that God would open the way for me to be a channel through which He could minister the Spirit-filled life to our people.

God was graciously providing me with the spiritual covering I needed. I had the blessing of my husband and then my pastor, even though I was new to that body. God is so good. He knew where to put me. Not all pastors accept women in public ministry but our pastor did, for which I thank God.

"Go...and tell how much the Lord has done for you, and how He has had mercy on you" (Mark 5:19; NIV).

15

HE WILL SHOW YOU...

The Holy Land! The very words stirred a longing in my soul to see the land where Jesus had lived, to walk where He had walked. When I heard about a planned tour of the Holy Land, I asked Bill if we might go.

"No," he said flatly. He must have seen my keen disappointment, for he added quickly, "Honey, when Pastor Fry leads a tour, then we will go."

One Sunday evening early in 1976, Pastor announced that in September his wife and he would be leading a tour to the Holy Land. My joy knew no bounds. I could hardly wait to get home and tell Bill. He was not feeling well, so he had stayed home from the evening service.

"Honey," I announced breathlessly, "now we can go to Israel because Pastor Fry is going to lead a tour in September!" Bill's face registered shock. "Remember," I went on, "you said that we would go when Pastor leads a tour."

"Me and my big mouth!" he groaned, but Bill is a man of his word and we made reservations for the trip. The timing of the tour was perfect, because we had recently celebrated Bill's retirement, which gave us more time and freedom in our lives. In May we left for ministry in Hawaii and returned the last day of June.

Then one morning in August, while in prayer, our Lord spoke to me and said, "Irene, I am going to show you the room where you saw Me that night in 1940. Go and tell the two pastors who are leading the tour."

"Do I have to, Lord?" I asked quickly.

His reply was simply, "Yes." It seemed like a very forward kind of thing to do, but I would obey the Lord.

My first appointment was with the associate pastor, Dale Daly. In sharing with him, I was led to sketch the stone building in the night vision—something I had never done before. He listened attentively and asked permission to keep the drawing.

"Would you tell Pastor Fry about it?" I asked.

"The Lord told you to tell him, not me," he replied gently but firmly. So, in obedience, I told Pastor Fry what the Lord had said.

"We'll see. We'll see," he said carefully.

I reminded him that in 1972 I had shared the experience with him. He remembered when I recalled to him that I had looked into Jesus' eyes. There was an ache in my heart because it seemed I was not being believed. I spoke to the Lord about it, reminding Him that He had told me to go to the two pastors and I had done so in obedience to Him. I remembered my husband's words when I had told him what the Lord had instructed me to do. Bill had said, "Wait until you get to Jerusalem and the Lord shows you the room; then tell them." But I had said, "No, the Lord told me to do it now." So I had.

When I got home, Bill asked if Pastor had believed me. I had to say, "I don't know. I don't think so."

The Lord wasn't through with me on this matter. A week later He told me to go back to the pastors and this time to be very specific telling them exactly how, when we got to the top of the stone stairway, we would turn left to walk on the porch and when we came to the door we would turn left to walk the length of the room.

Back I went and shared. Again Pastor Fry said only, "We'll see. We'll see." Pastor Daly just listened without comment.

It was the day before our departure when the Lord's words came to me clearly saying, "You are going to minister in Rome and you are going to sing, 'How Great Thou Art' in Hawaiian." Of all things!

"Yes, Lord," I answered, remembering that not only was Rome included on the tour but that we had a dear friend there who was a Roman Catholic Sister. I hurried to get the Hawaiian words to the song and to get them written on a back page of my Bible.

"Whatever are you doing, writing a Hawaiian song in your Bible?" Bill asked when he saw what I was doing.

"The Lord has just told me that I will be ministering in Rome and will sing this song," I told him. He replied with a shrug of his shoulders that said, "That's beyond me."

Departure day came at last. We were on our way to the Holy Land. We had been on the plane about two hours on the first leg of our trip when the Lord spoke to my heart, saying, "Go and tell Pastor Fry that you will be ministering in Rome and will be singing 'How Great Thou Art' in Hawaiian." Pastor's wife, Peggy, had left the seat beside him to speak to someone else, so I went and told him. Again, he said, "We'll see."

At that time, I couldn't understand why he kept saying, "We'll see." I thought he didn't believe me, but the truth of the matter was that he wanted to be sure that it was God speaking. What God speaks comes to pass. Actually, that is what God the Holy Spirit was teaching me, experientially, at that time. He is our teacher, as Scripture says, and I am so very thankful.

The tour took us first to Greece, then to Rome. When we got into our hotel, I called our Catholic Sister friend who was studying there. She came to see us at the hotel that evening and we introduced her to our pastors.

Before she left, she said, "Tomorrow evening we want to show you our convent and our hospital. Then we want you two to have dinner with us. By the way, Irene, we want you to minister tomorrow evening." We could only stand amazed.

The next evening she picked us up and took us to the convent where she was staying. We visited the hospital, and after dinner a group of Sisters gathered in their recreation room where God had me minister from 1 John 4 while our friend interpreted. After I had spoken, she turned to me and said, "Now, please, sing something in Hawaiian for us."

My dear husband turned pale as my two hands shot up in the air in praise to the Lord. And I sang, "How Great Thou Art" in Hawaiian with all my heart and soul. How great is our God and how true to His Word! What a joy it was to share all this with Pastor Fry the next morning.

From Rome we went to Jordan, to the Sea of Galilee and from there to Jerusalem. We came into the city by bus at sunset. A certain stillness seems to descend at that hour. It was a beautiful sunset, a lovely time to enter the Holy City.

Peggy Fry has been blessed with a beautiful voice and she was asked to sing "The Holy City" as we entered it.

The next morning was one of sightseeing, our second stop being at a place called "The Book" where the Dead Sea scrolls are kept. Inside, Pastor Fry began telling the group about the history of the scrolls. Peggy, having been there before, chose to sit and wait rather than follow along with him. The Spirit led me to go to her and tell her what the Lord had told me about seeing the room.

"Did Pastor tell you about the room the Lord has said He is going to show me?" I asked as we sat together.

"No," she said, "he didn't."

I then told her of the dream (as I called it) in 1940, and described the room. As she listened, her face suddenly lit up as though it had a bright light behind it. I wondered about it, especially after we both had gotten up from where we were sitting and moved to catch up with our husbands as the group moved out to board the bus. As she was speaking to her husband, the thought came to me: "She knows something I don't know." What she knew was the identity of the room in my dream.

Our next stop was the tomb of David. There was something about the area that stirred and excited me. The tour guide told us about the tomb and a rabbi also spoke to us briefly. It became increasingly difficult for me to pay attention to what they were saying, as the inner excitement mounted with a strange sense of urgent expectancy. Only later did I realize that it was God the Holy Spirit preparing me for what was coming.

"Follow me." I heard the guide's words and moved with the group as we followed him out, walked a short way, turned right for a short distance, then to the left. Bill, Peggy and I were trailing the rest of the group. As we turned that last corner I stopped stock still and stared in sheer amazement and awe. There in front of us was the stone building with the flight of stone steps on the outside wall **exactly** as I had seen it in the night vision.

"This is it, Honey, isn't it? This is it," Bill was saying. I could only nod my head, at a loss for words.

The rest of the group was already climbing the steps, the three of us still standing in a kind of courtyard where I had stopped to stare.

"Irene, aren't you coming?" someone called from the stairs.

I had been lost in wonderment. Oh, oh yes...go up the steps. As we got to the top of the stairs, sure enough, there was the porch with its stone floor just as I had seen it. We turned left down the porch a long distance 'til we came to the door where we entered and again made a left turn and descended a few steps into a large room, completely empty of furniture, the arrangement of the open windows, every detail, just as I had seen it.

A cry welled up from somewhere deep inside me. I turned and ran up against the wall, so overcome I could only sob uncontrollably. Peggy gently gathered me in her arms. The Spirit of God engulfed us both as we stood there trembling in awe and praising God.

Yes, this was the Upper Room, the room where Jesus and His disciples had their last supper (Passover) together. Now I understood why Peggy had been so radiant when I described the room to her. She **knew**. Truly, whatever God speaks He brings to pass. Whatever He reveals to us is truth.

Presently, I seemed to hear the Lord almost whisper, "Go and kneel where you saw Me." Half blinded by the tears streaming down my cheeks, I moved immediately to the window ledge where I had seem Him reclining.

"Jesus, I love You. Jesus, I love you." The words kept repeating themselves softly for several moments as I knelt there. When the rest of the group gathered together in a circle to pray, I knew I was to join them. We soon found ourselves singing "Hallelujah," our voices rising and falling in wave upon wave as we lifted our hearts to our Lord Jesus, so wonderfully present in our midst just then.

We were still singing, eyes closed, hearts lifted in love, when in a vision I saw a beautiful golden crown. It was a circlet, open in the center, consisting of twelve vertical points. At the tip of each point were three little finger-like projections. The crown was gold and yet

---

it was transparent! Just beneath the crown was a hand of golden light spread open above twelve bun-shaped loaves of bread of the same golden light.

The Lord gave me to understand that the twelve loaves are the twelve tribes of Israel. The hand is the hand of God which is still over them. The crown represents the sovereignty of God; one crown, one Godhead, complete unity without beginning and without end in God the Father, the Son, and the Holy Spirit.

The twelve vertical points around the crown represented the twelve apostles who are to judge the twelve tribes of Israel. The three little projections on the top of each point represented the triune nature of God who rules over all without partiality. He loves all alike. His hand is still extended over His chosen people, Israel. He has not forgotten them. Because of their hardness of heart, unbelief and disobedience, only a remnant of the millions of Jews will be saved. We, as Christians, have failed to pray for Israel as we should.

"Pray for the peace of Jerusalem; they shall prosper that love thee" (Ps. 122:6).

"Blessed is he that blesseth thee (Israel) and cursed is he that curseth thee" (Num. 24:9).

Jesus said that "repentance and remission of sins should be preached in His name among all nations, **beginning at Jerusalem**" (Luke 24:47).

Americans have sent missionaries all over the world with the exception of Israel. God is now speaking to us that we might pray as Paul prayed, "My brethren, my heart's desire and prayer to God for Israel is that they might be saved" (Rom. 10:1).

For the first time, Paul's prayer became my prayer. I had never before prayed for Israel. How I thank God for taking me to Israel, for letting me see the Upper Room and the fulfillment of the vision of 1940, for I have learned a truth: God's prophecies are to be fulfilled concerning the Jewish people and Israel. As believers, we too are God's chosen people, the spiritual Israel, and can identify with them in prayer as Daniel did when he prayed, "O Lord Hear! O Lord, forgive! O Lord, listen and act! Do not delay for Your own sake, my God, for Your city and Your people are called by Your name" (Dan. 9:19; NKJV).

Four days after we had visited the Upper Room, Bill and I received the following note from a member of the tour group.

Dear Bill and Irene,

The Lord gave me these words last Sunday in the Upper Room and I wanted to share them with you:

"Oh My children, do you know the burden that is on My heart for My people the Jews? Do you realize that someone must stand in the gap to pray for them? To pray that their eyes might be opened, to pray them into the kingdom? Wilt thou be that people? Wilt thou be that army of intercessors that will count the cost and pay the price that My lost sheep of Israel might know Me in all My fullness and recognize Me as their Messiah, too?

Oh My people, I love you, but other sheep I have who are not of your fold. Them also I must bring."

Thank you so much for the blessing you both have been in my life.

With much love,

Alice O'Brien

What a wonderful confirmation our Lord provided of the vision and also the understanding of it. Should I live to be a hundred, I shall never forget all that happened that day, nor shall I ever tire of telling of the merciful goodness and greatness of our blessed Lord Jesus.

"He will show you a large upper room" (Luke 22:12; NASB).

"Blessed be the Lord; for He hath shewed me His marvelous kindness in a strong city" (Ps. 31:21).

16

A "MUSIC LESSON"

As any parent knows, children are full of questions. As one of God's children, I'm often asking Him questions. In one of those asking times, His response went like this:

"Irene, when you play a stringed instrument and one string is out of tune it makes the whole instrument sound off-key, doesn't it? Even if the other strings are in tune?

"That is how it is with My children. They may be in tune, of one accord, with Me in three areas of their lives, but out of tune, out of order, in one. Because of one area of sin, the whole is not in accord with My will. All must be in harmony.

"Also, when a number are gathered together, some of whom are of one accord with Me but one or two are not, the group as a whole will not be in harmony. The off-key notes of the one or two will be discordant. It is the same way in praying together; the prayer is hindered if there is unconfessed sin in the lives of one or two."

The Lord continued teaching on this principle. In a symphony orchestra, the conductor can hear just one off-note among all the instruments and will promptly correct it. In like manner the Holy Spirit is our conductor and will promptly correct us as we yield ourselves (our wills) to His leading and so be in harmony with God's will. Then when we pray in one accord He will hear and answer our prayer. We will then be living in unity of mind and heart with our Lord Jesus Christ. Then mountains shall indeed be removed and cast into the sea when we pray—but only then. (See Mark 11:23).

When I shared this with my friend, Rosellen, she asked, "Irene, have you ever heard a symphony orchestra tune up before they started playing?"

"No, I never have," I said. So she described it to me, including some insights into spiritual parallels, which I want to share with you here, in her own words:

"One note is sounded with which all must be in tune. That note is 'A'. It is the first, the last, and the only one given. Interesting...Jesus said, 'I am Alpha ('A') and Omega, the beginning and the end' (Rev. 22:13). He is the one and only with whom each must be in tune to be in harmony with one another.

"It is the responsibility of each player to listen carefully to that single note, 'A', and to make sure his instrument is in tune with it. He is not responsible for anyone else's instrument, only his own. Likewise, it is the responsibility of each person to be rightly related to Jesus, in tune with the 'A'. Although we can learn from others, it's something no one can do for us.

"Stringed instruments require fairly frequent tuning although the adjustments are slight when the instrument is used regularly. Strings tend to go flat with long disuse. However, when a new string is put on, usually replacing one that has broken, it gets out of tune very easily until it has been sufficiently stretched or tempered.

"New Christians, too, usually find that more adjustments are needed early on than after they have become seasoned and matured, stretched and tempered.

"If life has gone a little flat and dull, or if there seems to be discord as soon as we 'come in,' some correction is probably called for. We need to listen to the Lord and make whatever adjustments are indicated...perhaps repentance or forgiveness or obedience, etc.

"We hear much these days about stress and about tension as being negative, undesirable elements in our lives. We need to understand the positive dynamics of tension. Our lives have much in common with the strings on an instrument. If there is no tension at all, the string is incapable of fulfilling the purpose for which it was designed; it is useless. On the other hand, if it is subjected to too much tension, it will initially sound sharp (cutting, sarcastic, critical). If the tension becomes excessive (hypertension), it may approach (or exceed) the breaking point—a 'nervous breakdown' may follow, or break-up of a marriage or just an explosion of temper. Pursuing this figure further, remember it is the player who tunes his own instrument, not the conductor. If the string is too tight, under too much tension, it is not the doing of the Holy Spirit; He is our helper, our teacher, our guide who **leads** us. Too much tension is generally our own doing, either what we ourselves apply or what we permit. It's hard to picture Jesus in a state of frustration or of hypertension. It just does not fit Him! And if we will, we can attune our hearts to His.

"The word for music in the New Testament is 'symphonia,' (our English word, symphony), a harmony of sounds, a concert of instruments. If you have ever heard symphony players warming up just before a concert, you would say most certainly you were hearing cacophony, not music. The instruments may all have been well-tuned, even playing in the same key and from the same score. Yet they were not producing music, 'symphonia', until they **all** came under the baton of the conductor—under the direction of the Holy Spirit, in the figure we are using.

"It may seem a little ridiculous to point out that there would be no music, no 'symphonia'—harmony of sounds, if everyone were playing the same note. Yet isn't that what we sometimes expect of others? Don't we sometimes take exception to those who don't 'sound' as we do?

"Separate parts are written for various instruments, each player reading his own part. The conductor, who may also be the composer, has the full score in front of him. He sees all the parts as a whole. This can readily be likened to the Scriptures. What we see in each part becomes an integral part of the whole under the Holy Spirit.

"All compositions make use of rests—some quite short, some very long, when no notes are being played by certain instruments. The rests are as much a part of the composition as the notes themselves. There are right times to be still, to be quiet. There are times to be still and know who God is and be strengthened in quietness and trust.

"With all that's said in the Scripture about singing and using instruments to make music to the Lord, it would seem that God takes much pleasure in it and has created many different instruments for His great celestial symphony."

Bill and Irene Lewers, 1985.

"Give thanks to the Lord with the lyre; sing praises to Him with a harp of ten strings. Sing to Him a new song; play skillfully with a shout of joy" (Ps. 33:2,3; NASB).

17

BURNING HEARTS

It was early afternoon on a mild Spring day in 1968. Our daughter, Diane, had just come in the back door after picking up my bed sheets when the front doorbell rang. Carefully I cracked the door open. The man I saw standing there was wearing an old, faded blue plaid shirt; his shapeless trousers were held up with a rope, his black shoes badly worn. He was carrying an old brown plaid sport coat over his arm, and a battered brown hat in his hand.

"I'm so hungry," he said. "Could you please give me a little something to eat? Just a little something?"

"I'd be most happy to give you something to eat."

There was such a soft look in his blue eyes. He didn't have the look about him of a bum or a drunkard. In spite of his shabby clothes, he was clean.

Diane had come to the door with me. Now as I closed the door and we turned to go into the kitchen, she said, "Mother, did you see?"

"His eyes?" I asked.

"Yes."

We quickly prepared two sandwiches, poured a tall glass of milk

---

and put them on a foil pan along with a small package each of potato chips and corn chips. I took them out to him. Holding the food, he looked at me and thanked me warmly.

"Please, sit down," I said.

He sat down on the sidewalk just in front of the door.

I closed the door and went to our coat closet. Seeing the two sport coats my husband had there, I took out the brown one to give to the man. I got a long-sleeved brown plaid shirt and a new pair of work socks. There were no trousers I could give him to go with it because he was much taller than Bill.

I laid the coat on the dining room table to fold it. In checking the pockets, I found two pennies in one of them and took them out.

Diane protested, "Don't do that, Mom." She then slipped a dollar bill into the pocket.

"I can't understand it," she mused thoughtfully. "I feel as though I would be willing to beg for this man, a perfect stranger."

I started to say, "Somehow, inside, my..."

"Heart burns." Diane finished the sentence for me.

"Yes," I said, "yes, my heart burns."

"It's strange. I feel the same way."

We stepped out the door to give him the clothes. "We're not rich people," I told him, "but we would love to share these things with you: a coat, a shirt, and socks. My husband is much shorter than you so we don't have any trousers that would fit you."

He looked up. Again there was that look in his eyes. It was such an open look, the eyes as guileless as a baby's.

"Thank you," he said. "Thank you for what you have done."

Diane's two little boys, eight-year-old John and five-year-old Ronnie, had run in from the back yard when the doorbell rang. They had then sat and talked with the man the whole time. Now, as I offered him more milk, he looked down at the boys, then met my eyes and said, "No, thank you, I have been given enough. Thank you." The look in his eyes begs description.

Diane and I went back in the house. Again she was saying, "I can't understand it—I would beg for him."

She moved into one of the bedrooms where she could watch him. She saw him hand the plate and tumbler to John saying, "Thank you. Thank you." She went into the front bedroom then to watch as he left walking straight and tall down the walk and around the corner out of sight.

Meanwhile, John had come around to where I was in the back of the house; his earnest little face lifted to mine.

"Grandma, I wish I was home. I would have given him my piggy bank with the hundred pennies in it."

Little Ronnie chimed in, "Me too, so he could buy some shoes."

"You didn't say that to the man, did you?" I asked.

"Oh, no," John assured me. "I wouldn't tell him that. That would hurt him and I would never want to hurt him."

John related how the man had emptied the crumbs from the bag of potato chips and corn chips into his hand and eaten them. John's eyes grew wide.

"Grandma, my heart burns."

"Me too," Ronnie echoed.

All of us had been strangely and deeply impressed by our visitor. Diane and I were especially touched by the fact that the boys had not heard us tell each other how our own hearts had burned within us, yet here were two little boys who had sat next to the stranger, who felt their own hearts burn and expressed it.

Who was this man? What brought him to our home? Our home is on a dead-end street, well away from the main thoroughfare. There are three duplexes before one comes to ours.

When Bill came home and I told him about our strange visitor, he at first chuckled, then began thinking of all the homes ahead of ours from the main street. Sure enough, when we checked, the man had not gone to any of our neighbors' homes. When we told them about him, they wondered aloud, "Why didn't he come to our house? I wonder who he is?"

In the thirteenth chapter of Hebrews, verse two says, "Do not neglect to show hospitality to strangers, for thereby some have entertained angels unawares." We were reminded, too, of the account in the 24th chapter of Luke, of the disciples on the Emmaus road who exclaimed to one another, "Did not our hearts burn within us while He talked with us...?"

Yes, we can only wonder.

"Do not neglect to show hospitality to strangers, for by this some have entertained angels without knowing it" (Heb. 13:2; NASB).

18

BLESSINGS IN OBEDIENCE

Typically, specific daily guidance as to how and where the Lord would lead me during the day has come without advance notice. That can make for some interesting times.

To illustrate—one day I was meditating on the Scriptures that were to be shared that evening at the first weekly Bible study in our home. While earnestly seeking the mind of the Lord concerning them, it seemed the Lord was saying to me, "Get up and go to (a certain store), to the book department there."

"Yes, Lord," I said, while thinking, "The Lord wants me to go check on all the various versions of the Bible. The people who are coming tonight will have different versions."

So I got ready and went to the designated store, making my way to the book department. I noticed a tall, young man standing there looking at the various Bibles, checking passage against passage. As I stood next to him looking at the Bibles, the Holy Spirit prompted me to speak to him. Now, how does one strike up a conversation with a total stranger?"

I said, "I can't, Lord. I don't know him."

Again the word came: "Speak to him."

"Lord, "I said, "if this is really You, have him lift his head and look at me."

No sooner had I prayed those words than the young man lifted his head, turned, and looked me full in the face. I was surprised, although I should not have been. (How often when we ask for something and the Lord grants it, do we gape in disbelief?)

Indicating the Bibles, I said, "You are wondering why different Bibles have the same Scriptures written a bit differently."

"Why, yes," he stammered in surprise. "How did you know that's what I was thinking?"

"I just knew," I told him. "The purpose is to make the Bible more understandable, but they mean the same thing."

We chatted a bit about that. He paused a moment, looked at me rather carefully, then said, "You know, I was at home just now feeling pretty disgusted with my life. What is there to life anyhow? I have everything I could want—like a nice home, car, boat, all those things— yet I really have nothing. Inside, well, there's nothing there. I'm empty." The look on his earnest face was clearly asking, "Can you possibly understand what I'm saying?"

Indeed, I did understand, and my heart went out to him. I simply said to him, "You need Jesus," then told him, "I was preparing for a Bible study in our home this evening when I felt clearly led to come to the book department here in this store to look at Bibles. I didn't know why, but I obeyed the leading."

We talked a bit further and he said, "When I was about eleven years old I went to Sunday school for a while. I thought the Bible was pretty interesting and would ask lots of questions in class. The teacher finally asked me to be quiet because I was asking too many questions and after a while I stopped going."

"How sad!" I exclaimed. "By all means start reading the Bible again. Pray for understanding and seek the Lord. Get into a church that preaches the whole gospel, one where you can find fellowship and grow. Why not come to our Bible study this evening? We would be so pleased to have you," I told him.

The young man did not accept my invitation and I never saw him again. I know that our meeting was a God-appointed one and trust that we shall meet again in heaven, for the Lord surely was drawing him to Himself. No one needs to remain "empty inside," for he can be filled with all the fullness of God when he knows the love of Christ which surpasses knowledge. (See Eph. 3:19).

I could easily have missed the Lord's quiet prompting to go to that store. Or, I could have dismissed it, perhaps doubting it was from Him, or considering it unimportant, or seeing it as too inconvenient that day. What a mistake that would have been. How much I would have missed! For there is always blessing in obedience. True, I don't have a "success story" to relate of seeing that young man find fulfillment and purpose for his life in Jesus, but I can trust God for continuing what He began that day.

When we walk in obedience, we actually have a part in the carrying out of God's purposes in our lives, some of which may touch others. And we know that God's purposes are always good.

"I am come that they might have life, and that they might have it more abundantly" (John 10:10).

103

19

BEHOLD, THE BRIDE

It was in that half-awake, half-asleep state early one morning, not long ago, that I saw myself in a church standing in the center aisle. There were people sitting in the pews on either side. There were men standing beside me in the aisle, who, I somehow knew, were priests.

Looking up, I saw that there was no ceiling, only the sky with some white clouds in it. In the midst of the clouds was an opening which appeared to recede to a great depth. Within the opening, I could see many people animatedly moving about.

"Look! Look!" I said excitedly to the man standing by me. They looked but saw nothing.

Forgetting the men, I looked back and watched as all the people disappeared. In their place a woman stood under a long golden canopy all in a flood of brilliant light. She was wearing a long-sleeved gown of what looked like a heavy, satin-like fabric, whiter than white, and so long it covered her feet. On her head was a lovely crown of solid gold, with no ornamental open work, which came to a peak at the very top. She was radiantly beautiful and looked very majestic, like a queen in a bridal gown.

For just an instant, I closed my eyes. When I opened them to look again, I noticed a little, bronze box by her feet. It was very small—no more than five or six inches long, three or four inches wide and about four inches high. The lid was not flat but rounded, like that of an old-fashioned trunk.

"What is in that box?" I asked.

Suddenly the vision was gone just as suddenly as it had appeared. Having become fully awake, I got out of bed and looked at the clock. It was 6:25 a.m. The Lord let me know that the vision had begun at 6:20 a.m. (Why that detail should have any importance, I do not know). In prayer I asked our Lord for understanding of the vision He had given.

Our daughter, Diane, called later that morning and I told her about it. Immediately she exclaimed, "Oh, Mother, that was the bride of Christ, the Church, that is being prepared for Jesus!"

"Oh! Why, yes, of course!" In my heart was that unmistakable "yes" and "amen." It had to be the Bride.

But I wanted a fuller understanding of the vision that I might know God's heart and whatever He would share with me. He has plainly said, "Ask and it shall be given, seek, and ye shall find, knock and it shall be opened unto you" (Matt. 7:7). So, in prayer, I asked. Some understanding came then, some came later. Actually, it's good that He doesn't tell us everything all at once. It's somewhat like a box of chocolates; each piece is a pleasure to be savored and enjoyed. Gobbling down the whole box at once would be more than we could handle, much less enjoy.

At that time God gave me to understand that the many people I had seen are the one bride of Christ, that the golden canopy and the brilliant light was the Shekinah glory all around her. Her whiter than white gown speaks of purity, of being cleansed, washed and saved by the blood of Jesus Christ in His love, mercy, and grace.

Later in the day, I told Rosellen about the vision. When I described the box, I said, "I don't know what it was."

"Oh, that's treasure! It's a treasure box, Irene," she said unhesitatingly.

"My spirit witnesses to that," I said. "Perhaps the Lord will give you some further understanding of the vision."

"I'll certainly let you know if He does," she assured me.

A day or so later Rosellen called. She had asked the Lord if there

---

was anything He might show her that would give us more understanding of the vision. She was wondering about the box in particular. Immediately, some words of a long-loved hymn she had not sung for years came to mind:

"So I'll cherish the old rugged cross
Till my trophies at last I lay down
I will cling to the old rugged cross
And exchange it some day for a crown."

"That's what it is, Irene. The treasure in the treasure box is trophies! And they were laid down right beside the Bride." She sounded very positive, confident, incredulous, and excited all at the same time. She went on to explain, "In all these years I never had considered the oddity of such a choice of words as 'trophies' in the chorus of that hymn. I looked in the dictionary to be sure my understanding of the word was accurate. It said that a trophy is any memorial of victory or conquest. Since these trophies are related to the cross of Christ, they are emblematic of every victory that is ours because of His on Calvary's cross."

"That's beautiful, just beautiful," I replied. "Now, isn't this something—when you said 'treasure' the other day, I must have mentally converted treasure to jewels and thought that is what you said. I went to the dictionary too, and found that meanings for jewel include 'a precious possession, a thing or person of great worth or excellence, a precious stone, a costly ornament'. Also, I was impressed that the left hand wasn't to know what the right hand was doing, that these jewels represented those things which were done unto the Lord alone, to be pleasing to Him not to men. For whatever is done for recognition by man has already brought all the reward there will ever be as He tells us in Matthew 6:3-5."

Is our God inconsistent? Does He give conflicting answers to different people? No, a thousand times, no! Our God is a God of order, of truth, of rightness...and wisdom. He intended for me to hear "jewels" when Rosellen distinctly said "treasure," for in a sudden flash of insight she understood and her words came in a rush.

"Why, of course, the treasure is the collection of trophies, the memorials of victories and conquests, the overcomings when we have truly won out over the world, over sin, over self, over Satan, over circumstances, having been made 'more than conquerors through Him who loved us' (Rom. 8:37). I'm just seeing that. Do you see it, Irene? The trophies are His jewels and they are **precious** to Him. **What are trophies to the Bride are jewels to the Bridegroom**.

"What could be more simple? Or beautiful? Or **profound?** It's also very sobering, isn't it? For whenever our righteous doings are tainted by the desire to be well thought of by men, there is nothing left to offer to Jesus, nothing that would be truly **all His**."

Both of us were silent as we pondered the same thing— wondering how often we deceive ourselves—how often we have mixed motives...desiring to please the Lord, but also desiring some personal recognition and approbation. Oh, that we might live our lives for Him and **only** for Him! How fitting that the box should be bronze, the metal which is figurative of the righteousness of God's judgment.

As the full realization hit me of what that little box represented, my heart simply broke and I cried out, "But Lord, it's so small! We're bringing you **so little** and You have given **so much!**"

Then I learned something about the canopy under which the bride was standing. A canopy is part of the traditional Jewish wedding ceremony even today and symbolizes the home to which the groom will take his bride. It is another beautiful truth in picture form of the glorious home our Lord has prepared for her, the New Jerusalem. The Scriptures even tell us that over all the glory will be a canopy (Isa. 4:5; NASB).

You have heard it said that a picture is worth a thousand words. Surely the truths God has communicated to me in picture form by way of visions such as this have spoken "volumes!" Perhaps He has "spoken" to you that way. Perhaps He has not. Either way, there is no room for pride or apology. We are literally surrounded with picture lessons through which any willing heart can be taught. Did not Jesus Himself use simple, everyday objects anyone could see as a means of teaching great truths? Remember such things as the yoke, the salt, the seed, the leaven, the bread, the shepherd, the door, the wheat, the tares, and so many more? The people had the written Word of God in the Holy Scriptures. Today, I, too, have the precious written Word of God, yet still am helped to understand it more clearly, and sometimes more personally, in the picture forms He has allowed me to have.

———

The Lord being our teacher, we will learn that every truth, every principle, in the realm of the natural will have a counterpart, a like truth, in the spiritual realm. As Andrew Murray has said, "All earthly things are shadows of heavenly realities. They are the expression in created, visible forms, of God's invisible glory. The Life and Truth are in heaven. On earth we have figures and shadows of these heavenly truths."[1]

Do I fully understand this figure of the bride of Jesus? Assuredly, I do not. But this I do know, that God's Word is true and that we who are His, the Church He loved and gave Himself for, must be ready when He comes. He is coming for a glorious Church without spot or wrinkle or any such thing, one that is holy and without blemish (Eph. 5:25,27). There will be no time for repentance and cleansing when, with the trumpet of God and a commanding shout, the Lord Himself will descend from heaven and we shall be caught up to meet Him in the air and so be with the Lord always (1 Thess. 4:16). All is in readiness in the heavenlies. The groom is waiting for God's perfect time.

One day, very soon, the trumpet will sound. The Bride, the Church, must be ready.

ARE YOU READY?

"Blessed is he that readeth, and they that hear the words of this prophecy, and keep those things which are written therein; for the time is at hand" (Rev. 1:3).

---

[1]*The True Vine* Andrew Murray, Whitaker Press, 1982, pg. 9.